GREAT CHEFS ®
of
Chicago

Also Available
GREAT CHEFS OF NEW ORLEANS II
GREAT CHEFS OF SAN FRANCISCO

Copyright ©1990 Great Chefs/1985 by
Tele-record Productions, Ltd.
Published by arrangement with the author
ISBN: 0-929714-03-02
Library of Congress Catalog Card: 85-47646

For information address Great Chefs Television Productions
P.O. Box 70677, New Orleans, LA 70172

Library of Congress Cataloging in Publication Data
Main entry under title:

Great Chefs of Chicago.

   1. Cookery, International. 2. Cooks—Illinois—Chicago.
I. Tele-Record Productions, Ltd.
TX725.A1G715   1985   641.5'09773'11   85-47646

Funding for THE GREAT CHEFS® OF CHICAGO has been
provided for by Duncan Hines Food Products Division of
The Procter & Gamble Company and by Harvard Cutlery from
True Value Hardware Stores

Printed in Hong Kong

DON 10 9 8 7 6 5 4 3

One of the implicit benefits of the GREAT CHEFS series is that the television programs illustrate the chef's style and technique absent from the written word of the accompanying cookbooks. The use of both the book and viewing the series can allow you to achieve ''chef-like'' results.

We feel it is important for you to understand that although it is not impossible to prepare these recipes from the book alone, viewing the TV series is more than helpful. THE BOOK AND SHOW ARE A PAIR.

The premises of the GREAT CHEF series (GREAT CHEFS OF NEW ORLEANS, NEW ORLEANS II, SAN FRANCISCO, and CHICAGO) are simple if not unique. First, we assume that the viewer/cookbook buyer knows *something* about cooking. Secondly, the series is not strictly a *recipe* program, but rather instructional cooking classes that allow a viewer the opportunity to watch professional chefs work through the preparation and cooking steps of a dish.

Each of these steps determines the success of the preparation of a recipe. For example, we often will carry a key cooking step much longer than the typical cooking show. One cannot learn to make a sauce or other complicated mixture without seeing the consistency and texture develop. If this process takes time in the kitchen, we generally take time on the show.

It is no secret to anyone interested in cooking that the working environment of a restaurant is light years away from the home kitchen. The equipment, food products, and staff make it a very different endeavor. In the course of producing shows with forty-one chefs, we have identified over fifty-two of their menues and hundreds of dishes with definitive moments when cooking in a restaurant kitchen will translate easily and pro-

ductively to the home kitchen. Although many of the chefs use gram measurements, we have converted these to ounces for your convenience and accuracy. By simply adding a moderately-priced food scale to your kitchen, you'll be ready to cook and much of the myth regarding pastry and desserts will evaporate.

Through watching the television programs you will pick up a wealth of knowledge about basic cooking techniques that apply to hundreds of recipes, inventive garnishes and facile presentation. Watch the television programs. They are important companions that bring to life the personalities, recipes and instructions in this book.

One final note regarding the recipes: The number of servings and the preparation times are listed for each dish. Certain recipes also include the phrase *note elapsed time.* This indicates that advance preparation is needed. Always read the entire recipes before planning your dinner.

Good luck and bon appetit.

CONTENTS

✗

GABINO SOTELINO
AMBRIA

For Spanish-born Gabino Sotelino, the lightness of the food at Ambria represents a total reversal of his philosophy of cooking. Rather than nouvelle cuisine, he terms his style *cuisine légère*—light cuisine—and conceives dishes according to what he sees on trips to the market, rather than having a set menu plan.

"All of my training was in classic cooking, but that isn't what people want anymore," he says. "I think about what people need to eat to be healthy. When my customers get up from the table I want them to feel filled, but still have the energy to go dancing."

Even rich dishes, such as lightly sautéed *foie gras*, are lightened with a garnish of diced fresh apple, and the ingredients for a pâté are wild mushrooms with morsels of fresh *langoustine*, rather than meats and fats.

Although the food Gabino serves is what he terms the "style of today," the setting for Ambria harkens to the elegance of art nouveau. Located off an apartment/hotel lobby in Chicago's Lincoln Park, diners enter to find deep brown wood walls lit by frosted wall sconces, brown leather banquettes and lush palms atop wooden stands in front of high windows curtained with white lace.

The dining room resembles those of the grand hotels in Europe where Gabino received most of his training, beginning in his native Madrid after leaving a monastery at age 7.

"I was a bellboy at the Ritz Hotel in Madrid when I was not even 13," he recalls. "After that, I started working in the kitchen as an apprentice."

Working through the various positions in the kitchen led Gabino to hotels around the world, including the Plaza Athenée in Paris, Koons Hotel in Switzerland, Hilton Hotels in Hong Kong, Istanbul, Tokyo and Montreal, as well as resort areas such as the Canary Islands and the French Riviera.

Although he now rejects the richness of the classic French style he once practiced, some of his tenets remain the same. "We did make everything from scratch," he says. "Nothing was from the can the way restaurants in this country used to make food. We churned our own ice cream, made all our tomato sauces from freshly peeled tomatoes and prided ourselves on *charcuterie*."

That style did, however, bring Gabino to the Madison Hotel in Washington, D.C., his first job in the United States and the last time he commanded a hotel kitchen. From there, he went on to the White House, later moving to Chicago to become chef at Le Perroquet and the Pump Room.

During his first years in Chicago he met restauranteur Richard Melman, who he convinced to join him on a trip through Europe to sample the kind of food he wanted to prepare at Ambria. "I wanted to create my own cuisine, and he had the money to back the operation." Three weeks and twenty-eight restaurants later, Melman became Gabino's partner.

Now, rather than using sauces to flavor many entrées—including a variety of fish flown in from around the world—Gabino relies on a combination of fruitwoods used in his grills. He will use as garnishes some of the herbs he plants in gardens in front of the restaurant; or a number of salads are made from raw and cooked vegetables, such as medallions of lobster he serves with three colorful *mélanges*.

But his best guides as to what to prepare and how to serve it are trips to the market. "It's only in the last few years that I can get everything we need right here in Chicago, and I never plan menus more than a few days in advance because I never know what I'll see there. Instead of set recipes, I let my eyes tell me what will be on my plate." ✗

AMBRIA
CHICAGO

MENU

CIGARETTES OF SMOKED SALMON WITH BELUGA CAVIAR
An artfully arranged hors d'oeuvre featuring rolled salmon and imported caviar

MOUSSE OF WILD MUSHROOMS WITH LANGOUSTINES AND AMERICAN CAVIAR
A creamy mousse served with sautéed langoustines and champagne butter rosé

LOBSTER WITH THREE SALADS
A fan of lobster medallions framed by dressed greens and matchstick vegetables

BREAST OF MALLARD ROTIS
Roast duck breast with Pinot Noir green peppercorn sauce, garnished with red cabbage

POACHED PEAR STUFFED WITH ICE CREAM
A palate-pleasing dessert combining fresh fruit, ice cream and chocolate

✘

8 ounces smoked salmon fillet
1 red onion, thinly sliced
1 lime, thinly sliced
2 chives
4 rose petals
2 hard-boiled egg yolks, chopped
4 tablespoons crème fraîche
4 ounces Beluga caviar
2 tablespoons small capers

Slice salmon into 4 thin sheets, about 2 ounces each. Roll each slice into a cigarette shape. Cut each into 2 equal pieces. In the center of each 10-inch serving plate, place 2 salmon ciga-rettes to form a V shape. Place 1 slice of onion on either side of the V. Place a slice of lime directly below each slice of onion. Chop chives in half and place one-half in the center of each V. Place a rose petal at the base of the V and top with the chopped egg yolk. Place a spoonful of crème fraîche in the center of the V, on top of the chive. Spoon caviar onto the crème fraîche. Sprinkle capers on the top portion of the plate, inside and around the opening of the V and serve.

WILD MUSHROOM MOUSSE
½ clove garlic, finely chopped
1 shallot, finely chopped
8 ounces cepes mushrooms, chopped
8 ounces shiitake mushrooms,
stemmed and chopped
(unstemmed chanterelle or morel
mushrooms may be substituted)
1½ ounces olive oil
2 tablespoons dry Madeira
2 tablespoons ruby port
2 eggs
4 tablespoons crème fraîche
dash of nutmeg
1 teaspoon sage
salt and pepper

In a large sauté pan, briefly sauté garlic and shallots in olive oil. Add mushrooms and sauté until brown. Season with salt and pepper. Flame with Madeira. Add ruby port, cover and reduce over very low heat until almost dry. Let mixture cool; then purée in a food processor with the eggs, crème fraîche, nutmeg, sage and dash of salt and pepper. Butter four 3- to 4- ounce timbale molds. Fill molds two-thirds full with mousse. Tamp on counter to remove air bubbles. Put molds in a larger pan partially filled with hot water and cover with foil. Bake at 325 degrees for 30 minutes. Remove pan from oven. Set molds aside to cool.

Mousse of Wild Mushrooms with Langoustines and American Caviar

CHAMPAGNE BUTTER ROSÉ
  2 shallots, finely diced
  2 cups rosé champagne
juice of ½ orange
juice of ½ lemon
10 seedless red grapes, stemmed and
    halved
  1 tablespoon heavy cream
½ pound cold unsalted butter
salt and pepper

Sauté shallots in a touch of butter.
Add champagne, orange juice, lemon
juice and grapes. Reduce until
syrupy; then add cream. Bit by bit
add remaining butter, agitating pan
constantly to incorporate. Season
with salt and pepper. Reserve, keeping warm.

ASSEMBLY
2 pounds whole fresh langoustines
    (approximately 20)
scant amount of olive oil
2 ounces small salmon roe
1 truffle, sliced
salt and pepper

Peel and devein langoustines. Sprinkle with salt and pepper and sauté
on both sides in olive oil barely covering the bottom of the pan. Unmold
the baked mousses and place one in
the center of each individual serving
plate. Place 5 langoustines around
each mousse pinwheel fashion.
Strain the champagne sauce over the
langoustines. Top each mousse with
a slice of truffle. Place salmon roe between the langoustines and serve.

4 cooked lobsters, 1-pound each
1 head red leaf lettuce
4 heads lamb's lettuce (mache)
12 ounces vinegar
8 ounces olive oil
½ pound French green beans,
    blanched
2 artichoke bottoms, braised or
    canned and cut into 2-inch long
    matchsticks
1 medium carrot, blanched and cut
    into 2-inch long matchsticks
2 medium black truffles, cut into 2-
    inch long matchsticks
salt and pepper

CASSIS DRESSING
  1 teaspoon Dijon mustard
juice of 2 lemons
juice of 1 lime
  3 tablespoons fresh black currants
    (or canned black currants in
    syrup)
  1 ounce white wine
  1 ounce black currant vinegar
¼ cup walnut oil
salt and pepper to taste
dash of Worcestershire sauce
    (optional)

Shell lobsters. Devein and cut each
tail into six medallions. Arrange lobster pieces in a fan shape on the lower
portion of serving plates. Place claw
meat on either side of the medallion
fan. In a bowl, toss the red leaf and
lamb's lettuce with salt, pepper, vinegar and olive oil to taste. Place the
dressed greens in the center of each
plate. In a bowl, toss the green beans
and artichokes with salt, pepper,
vinegar and olive oil to taste. Place
the artichokes on the upper right portion of the serving plate and the
green beans on the left. Toss the carrots and truffles with salt, pepper,
vinegar and olive oil to taste. Cross
hatch the truffles on top of the artichokes. Cross hatch the carrots on
top of the green beans. Spoon cassis
dressing (recipe follows) around the
lobster medallions and serve.

In a bowl, combine the ingredients
through the black currant vinegar.
While whisking, add walnut oil. Season with salt and pepper. Add Worcestershire sauce if desired.

BREAST OF MALLARD AND PINOT NOIR GREEN PEPPERCORN SAUCE

3 whole mallard breasts, with breast bone (from 2½ pound ducks)
8 cloves unpeeled garlic, blanched
1 shallot, finely chopped
1 sprig thyme
1 bay leaf
1 carrot, chopped
½ onion, chopped
2 stalks celery, chopped
3 mushrooms, sliced
2 ounces armagnac (available in wine stores)
½-¾ bottle Pinot Noir
2 cups duck stock
12 green peppercorns (canned)
1 teaspoon honey
salt and pepper

Heat a large ovenproof sauté pan until it smokes. Season both sides of the duck breasts with salt and pepper and place skin side down in the pan. Cook until skin is brown and crispy, turning occasionally. Add garlic cloves, shallots, thyme, bay leaf, carrot, onion, celery and mushrooms. Place pan with duck breasts skin side up in a 500 degree oven for 6 minutes until duck is medium rare.

Remove duck breasts from the pan and reserve, keeping warm. Remove the garlic cloves; peel and reserve (for garnish). Strain fat from and reserve remaining contents of the roasting pan.

Deglaze pan with armagnac. Add Pinot Noir; then put all the reserved strained seasonings and vegetables, except the garlic cloves, back in the roasting pan. Reduce liquid by three-fourths the volume. Debone the duck breasts and add the bones to the reducing sauce. When reduced, add the duck stock and peppercorns. Reduce again by one-half. Strain the sauce and add honey. Season with salt and pepper to taste. Reserve.

RED CABBAGE GARNISH

4 slices bacon, diced
½ head red cabbage, cored and julienned
salt and pepper

Heat a sauté pan. When very hot, add bacon and cook until crisp. Season cabbage with salt and pepper. Add the cabbage to the bacon; cover and cook until tender. Reserve.

POTATO BASKETS

2 medium Idaho potatoes, peeled and unrinsed
oil for deep-fat frying

Shred the potatoes into long thin strips. Line a potato basket mold with the potatoes overlapping and fry in 350 degree deep fat until golden brown. Unmold, drain and fill with blanched, sautéed fresh vegetables such as carrots, turnips, celery and zucchini.

Slice the duck breasts and serve approximately 1 to 1½ split breasts per person topped with the Pinot Noir sauce. Garnish with peeled, roasted garlic cloves, cooked cabbage, and potato baskets.

POACHED PEARS
2 cups water
2 cups white wine
2 cups sugar
peel from 1 lemon
peel from 1 orange
1 vanilla bean
4 medium-sized ripe sweet winter
  pears (Bosc or Anjou)

Put all the ingredients except the
pears into a saucepan and bring to a
boil. Peel; then core whole pears
through bottom (leaving stems on).
Add the pears to the saucepan; cover
and poach until soft (about 10 to 15
minutes depending on the ripeness
of the pears). Carefully drain or pat
dry the pears and allow to cool.

CHOCOLATE SAUCE
2 tablespoons butter
½ cup sugar
½ cup cocoa
¼ cup cream

Melt butter and add sugar and cocoa.
Stir until well blended. Add cream.
Bring to a boil and simmer for 5 min-
utes. Strain and reserve.

ASSEMBLY
1 pint ice cream, flavor of your choice
raspberry sauce (see page 101)
caramel sauce (see page 60)

Fill the pears with ice cream. Dip the
top half of the pear in raspberry
sauce. Dip the bottom half in caramel
sauce. Place a stuffed pear in the
center of each serving plate. Spoon
chocolate sauce around the pear. Decorate with melted white chocolate if
desired.

CAROLYN BUSTER
THE COTTAGE

When The Cottage opened in Calumet City more than a decade ago, chef/owner Carolyn Buster set as her standards the elegant atmosphere of Ferdinand Point's La Pyramide and fine food of Raymond Thullier's L'Oustau de Beaumanière.

But rather than being located in the rolling hills of Provence, her eighty-seat white stucco restaurant is on a main drag of an industrial area about twenty miles from Chicago, in a community with no history of fine dining.

What the 42-year-old, largely self-taught chef has done is create a personal restaurant with a style of cooking ranging from expertly handled basics (such as a schnitzel made with pork instead of veal) to woo locals to sophisticated dishes that garner awards and reviews that lure diners from the city. Her restaurant has been awarded four stars by the Mobil Travel Guide since 1978, and has been a Travel/Holiday Award winner since 1980.

The interior is as personal as the food

served there. Antique silver wine buckets and pitchers nestled in the wine rack are from travels to London's Portobello Road and the markets of Amsterdam. An antique oak bookcase, matching the assortment of chairs, is filled with part of her extensive cookbook collection. Topping one shelf is a glass-covered chef's hat signed by the likes of Pierre Franey from a "culinary cruise" aboard the *S.S. France*.

The building, with white lace curtains covering the bottom half of the windows, was modeled on the Relais de Campagne where Carolyn and her husband, Jerry— who studied wine and restaurant management before joining forces with his wife, and who now runs The Cottage's dining room— spent time during trips to France.

Her food, however, has developed its own style. While she admires the French, and believes a mastery of technique is essential, she also has been influenced by sources ranging from Louis Szathmary, chef of The Bakery where she first entered a restaurant kitchen, to an Indian descended from the Aztecs who taught her a method for smoking she now utilizes for poultry.

"People have an image of smoked foods being dry and salty, and my method is totally different," Carolyn says. "I stuff my poultry with celery, onions, apples and oranges, and then marinate it in apple cider and smoke it over a mixture of white oak and hickory. The result is totally moist, and the method works well with all poultry."

It was in 1969 that she acted upon her dream of owning a restaurant. "My sisters used to kid me when we would pass some greasy-spoon diner," she says. "They'd say, 'Look, that's Carolyn's restaurant!' "

"We couldn't survive without the local clientele," she says of running a restaurant in the culinary wilds of Chicago, "and didn't realize when we decided to have a serious restaurant in this area that the reason one didn't exist was there wasn't enough business. We thought of ourselves as missionaries."

Her menu, therefore, reflects both business sources. The Cottage schnitzel and The Cottage raspberry cake have been on her menu since the restaurant opened in 1974, and her customers want them to remain firmly in place. However, diners who glance at the framed blackboards listing the evening's specials will see anything from a rack of lamb with a light tarragon sauce to veal topped with slivers of onion and smoked breast of *poussin* with a sweet garlic sauce.

"I sometimes feel bad for Carolyn," says Jerry. "It's like there's a lid on her creativity." But Carolyn, who changes the menu every six weeks, takes satisfaction from meeting the standards she sets for herself—as high as a Mont Blanc—and from creating new dishes. "We continue to travel and that adds new influences to my food." ✗

THE COTTAGE
CALUMET CITY

MENU

SMOKED DUCK
*Marinated duck flavored with an Aztec-influenced spiced butter,
served with smoked garlic sauce*

SEA SCALLOPS IN SPINACH LEAVES
Spinach-wrapped large sea scallops with Tarragon Beurre Blanc Sauce and American caviars

"THE COTTAGE" SCHNITZEL
Chef Buster's delicious version of schnitzel, done with pork tenderloin

"THE COTTAGE" RASPBERRY CAKE
A variation of an English "summer fool" prepared with bread, butter, sugar and raspberries

CHOCOLATE RUM TERRINE
A moist chocolate cake served with a trio of chocolate mousses and chocolate rum sauce

✗

SMOKED DUCK

SERVINGS: 16 APPETIZER PORTIONS OR 8 ENTREE PORTIONS
PREPARATION TIME: 4 HOURS (NOTE ELAPSED TIME)

SPICED BUTTER
  2 pounds soft butter
  2 shallots, minced
6-8 cloves garlic, minced
  1 tablespoon parsley, chopped
  *1 tablespoon black peppercorns,
    crushed*
  2 teaspoons salt
  1 teaspoon chili powder
  ½ teaspoon oregano
  ½ teaspoon ground cumin
  ¼ teaspoon ground coriander
  1 teaspoon curry powder
  1 teaspoon dried basil
*few dashes each of Worcestershire and
    Tabasco sauces*

Blend all the ingredients in a food processor until well incorporated. Reserve at room temperature.

Smoked Duck

MARINADE AND DUCK
4 ducks, 4 to 4½ pounds each (see
  note below)
2 cups celery, chopped
2 cups onions, chopped
2 cups carrots, chopped
2 cups unpeeled tart apples, chopped
2 cups unpeeled oranges, chopped
1 large bunch parsley, chopped
1 gallon apple cider
4 whole heads garlic
corn oil

Generously rub inside and outside of
ducks with some of the spiced butter.
Mix celery, onions, carrots, apples,
oranges and parsley. Pack cavity of
each duck with this mixture. Using

the remaining spiced butter, place a
large dollop inside each. Stand ducks
tail-end up in a stainless or plastic
container (a large bucket works well)
and pour cider over. Add weight if
necessary to hold ducks submerged
in marinade. Marinate refrigerated
for 16 to 24 hours. Reserve marinade.

Preheat smoker to low to medium
range following manufacturer's sug-
gestions. Arrange some water-soaked
hickory, mesquite, or osage wood
chips over lava rocks (for more even
heat distribution). Place drip pan in
position and fill two-thirds with
some of the marinating liquid. Position ducks on rack above drip pan,

(continued)

breast side out and tail end up. Dip whole heads of garlic in corn oil and place in center of the rack with ducks.

Smoke for approximately 2½ hours to medium rare; after 30 minutes turn ducks so the breasts face in. It may be necessary to rotate ducks during smoking if smoker has "hot" spots. Remove ducks and hold in warm place. Remove and peel garlic cloves. Reserve juice in drip pan.

SMOKED GARLIC SAUCE
  4 cups smoking juices (add reserve
    marinade to equal 4 cups of liquid
    if short on juices)
  2 ounces smoked garlic cloves, peeled
    and puréed
  ⅛ teaspoon ground ginger
  ¼ teaspoon ground cinnamon
pinch of ground cloves
  2 bay leaves
  ½ teaspoon salt
  ¼ teaspoon white pepper
  1 cup currant jelly
  ⅔ cup port
  2-3 tablespoons cornstarch

Allow the smoking juices to settle; then skim and reserve fat. Strain juices through a strainer lined with a wet cloth. Put the strained juices in a saucepan and add remaining ingredients through currant jelly. Simmer 15 to 20 minutes; then thicken with mixture of port and cornstarch. Strain the sauce.

Sauté the remaining smoked garlic cloves in reserved fat until golden brown. Strain fat off garlic. Remove stuffing and debone the ducks (reserve stuffing and carcass). Thinly slice the duck breasts, rewarming in sauce if necessary.

Arrange the sliced duck breast on a serving plate. Spoon sauce over and around slices; garnish with sautéed garlic cloves.

Remaining marinade and strained drippings, along with the duck carcass and stuffing, can be simmered to prepare stock. The leg meat can be used for warm duck salad or soup.

Note: This dish can be prepared with fewer ducks as long as the other ingredients are adjusted accordingly. The fewer ducks smoked, however, the greater the heat intensity will be per duck. For slower, more even smoking and better end results, the chef recommends using 4 ducks.

SEA SCALLOPS IN SPINACH LEAVES

SERVINGS: 6
PREPARATION TIME: 45 MINUTES

TARRAGON BEURRE BLANC SAUCE
3 large shallots, minced
1 pound cold butter
2 tablespoons tarragon leaves,
  chopped
2 ounces tarragon vinegar
2 cups white wine
4 ounces crème fraîche
salt and white pepper

Sauté shallots in 2 tablespoons butter. When translucent, add tarragon leaves, vinegar and wine. Reduce to approximately ½ cup liquid. Bit by bit, whisk in remaining butter. Once all butter is incorporated, add crème fraîche. Season to taste with salt and white pepper. Remove from heat and keep warm.

(continued)

14

SCALLOPS

2 tablespoons butter
6 large sea scallops, approximately
   2 ounces each
12-18 large spinach leaves, stems
   removed and quickly blanched in
   salted boiling water
3 ounces each American sturgeon
   caviar, whitefish golden caviar and
   red salmon caviar

Heat butter in sauté pan until it starts to brown. Sear scallops, turning to seal all edges. Do not thoroughly cook. Remove, drain and cool. Encase each scallop in 2-3 spinach leaves. Fifteen minutes before serving, lightly butter a shallow ovenproof dish or sauté pan. Cover bottom with a small amount of Tarragon Beurre Blanc Sauce, and add the spinach wrapped scallops. Cover dish with buttered parchment paper and place in 450 degree oven for approximately 8 to 10 minutes, until hot.

Spoon some sauce on each warm serving plate. Place one scallop on top, and garnish with a rounded spoonful of each caviar.

SERVINGS: 4-6
PREPARATION TIME: 30 MINUTES

"THE COTTAGE" SCHNITZEL

2 large eggs
2 tablespoons flour
2 tablespoons Parmesan cheese,
   grated
½ cup milk
salt, white pepper, nutmeg and
   chopped parsley according to taste
2 pounds pork tenderloin, trimmed
   of all fat and silverskin
flour to dredge
8 ounces butter
3 ounces lemon juice (for less
   tartness, dilute with orange juice
   or white wine)

Blend ingredients through seasonings in blender at high speed for about 2 minutes to form a batter. Slice tenderloin into ¼- to ½-inch thick pieces (depending on the size of the tenderloin) and pound into 3-inch, thin medallions. Dip each medallion in flour; then place in batter.

Melt enough butter to cover bottom of a large, heavy frying pan. Place medallions in pan so that they don't touch each other. Sauté until completely browned on one side; then loosen with a spatula and turn to cook the other side. Remove to a serving tray and quickly deglaze frying pan with lemon juice. Briefly reduce liquid to form a thick glaze. Strain the glaze over the schnitzels and serve immediately.

"THE COTTAGE" RASPBERRY CAKE

SERVINGS: 16
PREPARATION TIME: 20 MINUTES (NOTE ELAPSED TIME)

1½ pounds day-old French or Vienna
 bread
1 pound room temperature butter
2 cups sugar
6-8 cups frozen raspberries with
 juice, defrosted
1 quart sour cream sweetened with
 2 tablespoons light brown sugar
 (crème fraîche may be
 substituted)

Butter the inside of a 10-inch mold, that is approximately 3 inches deep, and dust with sugar. Remove crusts and then slice bread approximately ½-inch thick. Butter one side of bread slices and line bottom and sides of the mold, pressing buttered side of bread to dish.

  Generously smooth additional butter over bread-lined mold. Sprinkle with approximately ½ cup sugar. Add half the raspberries and juice; sprinkle with another ½ cup sugar; add another layer of buttered bread. Smooth additional butter on the bread; layer with more sugar and raspberries as before. Finish with a layer of buttered and sugared bread. Cover mold with plastic wrap and place a flat plate or baking sheet on top; weight down evenly and chill on a tray in refrigerator for six hours to overnight. To serve, unmold by wrapping hot damp towels around mold and inverting onto a serving plate. For extra color, pour any remaining strained raspberry sauce over top and sides of cake. Serve with sweetened sour cream. Garnish with whole fresh raspberries if desired.

CHOCOLATE RUM TERRINE

SERVINGS: 12-15
PREPARATION TIME: 2½ HOURS

TERRINE
8 ounces bittersweet chocolate,
 chopped (slightly sweetened dark
 chocolate available in specialty
 stores)
1 teaspoon Swiss coffee paste or 1
 ounce chocolate mocha bean candy
1½ ounces prepared strong coffee
8 ounces room temperature sweet
 butter
8 large eggs, separated
3 ounces all-purpose flour
8 ounces sugar
3 ounces strong dark rum
 (Baczewski Tea-Rum, if available)
½ teaspoon salt

Preheat oven to 350 degrees. Butter a 12-by-4-by-4-inch ovenproof terrine or two standard loaf pans and line bottom with buttered waxed paper. Combine chocolate, coffee paste or candy, and coffee. Melt together and when smooth, stir in butter. Beat egg yolks until light and fluffy, gradually adding sugar, flour, and rum. Stir egg yolk mixture into melted chocolate. Beat egg whites with salt until stiff. Quickly fold together chocolate batter and beaten egg whites. Pour into prepared terrine.

  Set terrine in larger pan and pour hot water to reach halfway up the sides of terrine. Bake approximately 90 minutes, or until firm. Cool to room temperature. Invert; remove from terrine and peel off waxed

(continued)

paper. Chill; will keep for 1 or 2 days in the refrigerator.

WHITE CHOCOLATE MOUSSE

2 envelopes (¼ ounce each)
   unflavored gelatin
1 cup milk
1 pound white chocolate, chopped
2 teaspoons lemon juice
zest (pith-free peel) of two oranges,
   grated and rinsed in very hot
   water
2 ounces Grand Marnier
4 egg whites
2 cups whipping cream

Soften gelatin in milk; then combine with white chocolate. Melt together, stirring occasionally. Add lemon juice, orange zest, and Grand Marnier. Stir over an ice water bath a few minutes to cool and firm. Beat egg whites until firm and fold into chocolate mixture. Whip cream into soft peaks and fold into chocolate. Chill in refrigerator.

MILK CHOCOLATE MOUSSE

1 pound milk chocolate, chopped
2 ounces prepared strong coffee
4 egg yolks
2 ounces Bailey's Irish Cream
2 teaspoons lemon juice
2 egg whites
1 cup whipping cream

Combine chocolate and coffee. Melt together, stirring occasionally. Beat egg yolks until light and thick. Stir yolks into melted chocolate; then add Bailey's and lemon juice. Stir mixture over an ice water bath to cool and thicken. Beat egg whites until firm and fold into chocolate mixture. Whip cream into soft peaks and fold into chocolate. Chill mousse in refrigerator.

DARK CHOCOLATE MOUSSE

1 pound bittersweet chocolate,
   chopped
4 ounces prepared strong coffee
4 egg yolks
2 ounces Tia Maria
2 egg whites
1 cup whipping cream

Combine chocolate and coffee. Melt together, stirring occasionally. Beat egg yolks until light and thick. Stir yolks into melted chocolate, then add Tia Maria. Stir mixture over an ice water bath to cool and thicken. Beat egg whites until firm and fold into chocolate mixture. Whip cream to soft peaks and fold into chocolate. Chill mousse in refrigerator.

CHOCOLATE RUM GLAZE & SAUCE

 3 cups sugar
 1 cup good quality cocoa
 2 cups water
16-30 ounces butter, cut in pieces
   (flavor and shine increase with
   additional butter)
½ cup strong dark rum (Baczewski
   Tea-Rum, if available)
¼ cup brandy
¼ cup cognac

Combine sugar, cocoa, and water in heavy saucepan. Bring to a low boil; then simmer, stirring frequently, for 10 to 15 minutes until mixture is thick enough to coat the back of a spoon. Remove from heat and stir in butter. Reserve 1 cup for glazing terrine. Add rum, brandy, and cognac to remaining chocolate mixture. Let cool to room temperature.

Pour reserved glaze over the terrine. On each serving plate place 1 slice of terrine and surround with a scoop of each of the three mousses. Ladle chocolate sauce on the plate to surround terrine and mousses. Garnish with fresh strawberries, mint leaves and whipped cream, if desired.

MICHAEL FOLEY
PRINTER'S ROW

While drawing inspiration from American regional foods usually leads chefs to the bayous of Louisiana or the mesas of the Southwest, Michael Foley, owner of Printer's Row, is creating a sophisticated cuisine based on the staples of American home cooking. He then makes it part of the framework of Chicago by drawing ingredients from the baker's dozen of ethnic groups which comprise the city.

Michael's style and contributions were recently recognized by *Cook's Magazine*, which chose him as one of fifty for their first "Who's Who of Cooking in America." The 32-year-old chef was listed with the likes of the late James Beard and Julia Child.

But his age and youthful appearance belie the fact that he has been around kitchens all his life. Michael is a third-generation restauranteur; his restaurant and style are a departure from Ray Foley's, the restaurant opened by his grandfather in 1935, where he received a series of unofficial apprenticeships during his teenage years.

18

Although Michael knew he loved the restaurant business, he investigated careers including medicine while an undergraduate at Georgetown University, while continuing to work in restaurants. "Washington was a cosmopolitan city to me, and I'd eat everywhere and picked up a lot of flavors that way."

After graduation, he moved in 1975 to Ithaca, New York, to study for a master's degree in hotel management. It was while working at L'Auberge du Cochon Rouge, a restaurant in a small farmhouse owned by a French chef, that he made his commitment to the kitchen.

Returning to Chicago in 1977, Michael started working for small, individual restaurants, learning about the suppliers in the city. During these years, he traveled frequently to France, and visited with Paul Bocuse, Alain Chapel and other famous French chefs.

"The French reinforced the importance I place on technique, and the place for the individual restaurant. But in Chicago most restaurants were concepts, owned by large commercial firms. I had to investigate all parts of the city to find a space I could afford."

Printer's Row is marked by a maroon-and-white striped awning in a fading brick building and an area of the city Michael termed "blighted" when the restaurant opened in 1981. Like his food, the interior of the dining rooms is sophisticated yet casual, with earth-tone print valances and burgundy patent leather chairs adding color, and pewter service places giving the space a somewhat country look. There are framed prints of equestrian scenes and a carved wooden cow's head for decoration. A central pillar covered in white tile provides a serving area.

Diners know they can come often for dinner without repetition, as Michael changes at least 80 percent of his menu each week—beginning with a session at his computer on Sundays, when the restaurant is closed. He reviews the notes he has entered for dish concepts and determines which will be actualized and which techniques would be appropriate.

His emphasis on techniques and their importance is why he created a dish such as Veal Done Six Ways. "It's one of the animals that has parts appropriate for almost all cooking methods, and I wanted to show that," he says.

For other dishes, Michael starts by visualizing the entire plate, taking into account texture, flavor, aroma and color. "I like to combine a little bit of opposites on a plate, and I don't want anything to overpower anything else. I am committed to keeping food healthy." ✗

PRINTER'S ROW
CHICAGO

MENU

WILD MUSHROOMS FLAVORED WITH PINE NEEDLES
A large, full-flavored wild mushroom marinated in soy and dashi, baked with pine needles for aroma and flavor

NEW YORK DUCK LIVER TERRINE
Special-fed duck liver layered with white truffles and salami

FLUKE AND DAIKON
Scallopini of fish wrapped with daikon sheets, gently warmed with an aromatic vegetable broth

VEAL DONE SIX WAYS
Separate veal cuts cooked with distinctive techniques, joined in flavor by braising juices

MACAROON MOCHA BUTTERCREAM CAKE
A simple chocolate génoise enhanced by a different style of buttercream and a macaroon crunch

✗

SERVINGS: 4
PREPARATION TIME: 15 MINUTES

4 brown Vail mushrooms (any hearty wild mushroom may be substituted)
1 tablespoon dried dashi
1 teaspoon soy sauce
2 teaspoons sweet saki (Mirin)
1 teaspoon regular saki
pine needles

Gently clean mushrooms. Combine dashi, soy sauce and both kinds of saki to form a marinade. Brush mushrooms with marinade until soaked. Put a layer of pine needles in an ovenproof pan. Set the mushrooms on the pine needles. Pour some of the marinade on top of the mushrooms. Bake in a 400 degree oven for 4 to 5 minutes. Turn once while baking. To serve, cut mushrooms in half and present with a few fresh pine needles.

Wild Mushrooms Flavored with Pine Needles, Fluke and Daikon, and New York Duck Liver Terrine

SERVINGS: 6-8
PREPARATION TIME: 30 MINUTES (NOTE ELAPSED TIME)

TERRINE
 1 pound New York State duck liver
½ dozen Oregon truffles, sliced
¾ tablespoon salt
½ teaspoon pepper
dash nutmeg
½ teaspoon saltpeter
12 slices light garlic sausage, paper
   thin
 2 ounces chicken or duck fat

Soak livers for 2 hours in tepid water (not over 100 degrees). Drain. Separate each lobe of the liver. Remove veins and membranes. Dry liver.

Combine spices. Put half of the liver into a 4-by-8 inch earthenware terrine. Sprinkle with mixed seasonings. Stud liver with truffles. Top with a layer of sliced sausage. Season again; then add another layer of sausage. Fill terrine with remaining liver and season lightly. Press ingredients firmly together. Top with a thin layer of chicken or duck fat. Cover terrine and set in a larger pan filled with hot water. Place in a 400 degree oven. Turn heat off and leave terrine in oven for 25 to 30 minutes. Remove terrine and cool in refrigerator for 2 days.

BRAISED CELERY GARNISH
1 bunch celery
1 quart vegetable stock (without
    celery)
1 bay leaf

Cut celery into 6-inch stalks. Trim
outside with peeler to remove
strings. Arrange a single layer in a
pan and cover halfway with vegetable stock. Add bay leaf. Cover and
cook over medium heat until tender.
Cool in the stock. Drain and reserve
liquid from the celery.

VINAIGRETTE
¼ cup vegetable stock (reserved from
    celery garnish above)
2 tablespoons safflower oil
2 tablespoons white tarragon
    vinegar
fresh tarragon to taste
pepper to taste
salt if needed

Put all of the ingredients in a jar.
Shake well before using.

Allow the terrine to reach room
temperature before serving. Slice and
place one piece on each serving plate.
Garnish with braised celery dressed
with vinaigrette. Serve with warm
brioche if desired.

FLUKE AND DAIKON

SERVINGS: 4
PREPARATION TIME: 30 MINUTES

1 daikon (Japanese radish)
½ teaspoon salt
4 ounces fluke (flounder) fillet
4 tablespoons leek, julienned
4 pea pods, julienned
8 sprigs curly parsley
4 tablespoons potato, julienned
12 drops raspberry vinegar
soy sauce to taste
12 ounces vegetable stock (see note
    below)
4 tablespoons radish sprout
1 dash shichimate (Japanese 7 spice)

Peel the daikon and cut into a 6-inch
piece. With peeler, shave one
2-by-6-inch section per person. In a
bowl, salt the daikon and let sit about
15 minutes, until pliable. Skin the

fluke and cut 4 thin slices. Lightly
pound into scallopini. In a pan, combine the leek, pea pods, parsley, potato, raspberry vinegar and soy
sauce. Add the vegetable stock and
simmer. Drain the daikon and wrap
around the fluke, forming a rosette
shape. Top each fish rosette with radish sprouts and place in individual,
ovenproof serving bowls. Warm in a
300 degree oven for 3 to 4 minutes.
Add the shichimate to the simmering
vegetables and bring them to a boil.
Remove the fluke from the oven. To
serve, pour hot broth over the fluke
and garnish with the vegetables.
    Note: Use leftover stock from the
New York State Duck Terrine on page
21, adding bay leaf and thyme to
taste.

VEAL SAUSAGE (makes 12 3-ounce sausages)

1 pound veal, in 1-inch cubes
1 pound fatback, in 1-inch cubes
1 tablespoon salt
6 peppercorns, crushed
2 teaspoons fresh ground pepper
½ medium onion, chopped
1-3 tablespoons fennel
2 cloves garlic, chopped with center stem removed
2 ounces clarified butter
⅓ cup bourbon
pork casings

Combine veal and fatback. Add salt, crushed peppercorns and fresh ground pepper. Sauté the chopped onion, fennel and chopped garlic in 1 ounce clarified butter until the onions become transparent. Remove onion mixture from heat; drain and cool. Pour the bourbon over the veal and fatback; then add the cooled onion mixture. Marinate in the refrigerator for 2 days; then put into casings to make sausages.

Poach the sausage in water to 140 degrees. Drain and dry; cook over medium heat in 1 ounce clarified butter until brown. Keep warm while preparing the rest of the veal.

VEAL SHANKS

4 1-inch center-cut veal shanks, at room temperature
4 tablespoons clarified butter
4 tablespoons olive oil
2 onions, chopped
1 stalk celery, chopped
2 carrots, peeled and chopped
3 cloves garlic, center stem removed
1 tablespoon tomato paste (optional)
1 pinch of dried thyme
1 bay leaf
2 sprigs parsley, chopped
½ teaspoon peppercorns
4 cups chicken stock
1 cup veal stock
1 tomato, peeled, seeded and chopped
1 ½-ounce piece of ginger, minced
2 leaves fresh basil, julienned
salt

Heat an ovenproof sauté pan. Add the clarified butter and olive oil. When they are hot, salt the shanks and put them in the pan to brown. Add the chopped onion, celery, carrots, garlic, and tomato paste (if desired). Add the herbs. When the meat is brown on both sides, remove from pan and reserve in a warm place.

(continued)

23

Briefly sweat the vegetables. Add the chicken and veal stocks. Bring the stocks to a boil and reduce by one-third. Put the shanks back into the pan and add the chopped tomato and ginger. Place the pan in a 350 degree oven for 20 minutes. Turn the shanks and roast until the meat is tender, approximately 35 minutes. Remove the shanks from the roasting pan and reserve in a warm place, covered. Reduce the roasting juices to 2 cups. Add the fresh basil. Purée all the vegetables and herbs with the juices in a food mill. Reduce again if necessary. This sauce may be buttered if desired. Reserve shanks and sauce until service.

GRILLED VEAL TENDERLOIN
4 veal tenderloin pieces, 2 ounces
  each
2 tablespoons olive oil
pinch of basil
pinch of bay leaf
pinch of thyme
pinch of garlic, chopped
pinch of peppercorns, crushed
pinch of parsley, chopped
salt and pepper to taste

Season the tenderloin pieces with salt and pepper. Combine the olive oil with the remaining ingredients to make an herb oil. Coat the tenderloins with the herb oil and grill about 10 minutes, to medium-rare or medium according to preference. Reserve, keeping warm.

VEAL SWEETBREADS
12 ounces veal sweetbreads
 4 tablespoons clarified butter
 4 tablespoons olive oil
 4 tablespoons shallots, chopped
 1 cup cucumber, julienned
12 ounces chicken stock
salt and pepper to taste

Season the sweetbreads with salt and pepper. Lightly brown sweetbreads in butter and oil in an ovenproof sauté pan. Add shallots and cook for 30 seconds. Add the cucumber and chicken stock. Cover and put in a 400 degree oven for 5 to 7 minutes, turning occasionally. Remove from oven and reserve while finishing the rest of the dish.

VEAL KIDNEYS
8 ounces veal kidneys
4 tablespoons clarified butter
4 tablespoons olive oil
4 cloves garlic, minced
2 shallots, mined
salt and pepper to taste

Cut kidneys to portion for sauté. Season with salt and pepper. Sauté to medium rare in butter and olive oil with the garlic and shallots, tossing gently. Drain and reserve.

VEAL MEDALLIONS
4 veal medallions, 2 ounces each
salt and pepper to taste

Brown the veal medallions on both sides in a nonstick pan (use no oil or butter). Cook until lightly pink.

On heated serving plates, put a portion of each of the six veals. Add some of the braising liquid from the sweetbreads to the veal shank sauce. Ladle the sauce over all the veal and serve.

CHOCOLATE GÉNOISE
1 ounce unsalted butter
1 heaping tablespoon cocoa
3½ ounces cake flour
6 eggs
5 ounces sugar
zest (pith-free peel) of 1 orange,
grated

Melt butter. Sift cocoa and cake flour together. Break eggs into a separate mixing bowl and add sugar. Whisk over warm water just until warm; then whip with a mixer at high speed until cool, light in consistency and almost doubled in volume. Fold in flour mixture; fold in butter and orange zest. Pour into a buttered and floured 6-inch springform pan. Bake in a 350 degree oven for about 30 minutes. When cool, cut into 3 layers.

MOCHA BUTTERCREAM
6 eggs
10 ounces sugar
2 ounces expresso (strong coffee may
be substituted)
8 ounces unsweetened chocolate,
melted
7 ounces room temperature butter,
cut into 1-inch cubes

In the top of a double boiler, whisk together eggs and sugar over heat until mixture becomes fluffy and triples in volume (bubbles will disappear and it will become a thick cream). Remove from heat and add the expresso and melted chocolate. Whip at high speed with a mixer until cooled (about 7 to 10 minutes). Gradually add butter and whip 3 to 4 minutes until butter is incorporated. Reserve at room temperature.

SYRUP
2 ounces water
1 ounce sugar
2 drops orange liqueur

Bring water and sugar to a boil. Remove from heat and add orange liqueur. Reserve at room temperature.

GANACHE
6 ounces semi-sweet chocolate
6 ounces unsweetened chocolate

Combine ingredients and slowly melt over warm water. If mixture seems too thick, add 1 tablespoon water. Reserve at room temperature.

ASSEMBLY
1 cup ground chocolate macaroons
2 blood oranges
mint leaves

Into a 6-inch springform pan place 1 layer of chocolate génoise. Baste cake with half the syrup. Pipe a layer of buttercream onto cake. Sprinkle with ground chocolate macaroon. Press down on the layers. Repeat with another layer of génoise, the remaining syrup, buttercream and ground macaroons. Top with the third layer of génoise. Spread ganache on top. Refrigerate overnight. Unmold and, if desired, pipe additional buttercream on the top and spread on the sides of the cake. To garnish, press additional ground macaroons onto the sides. Let stand to room temperature.

Serve with blood orange sections and mint leaves.

PIERRE POLLIN
LE TITI DE PARIS

Most French chefs replicate the patterns of their past, including an autocratic sense of power in their kitchens. But the superb nouvelle cuisine produced by Pierre Pollin at Le Titi de Paris in suburban Palatine proves that tension is hardly necessary for quality.

"I never scream, and I like a quiet happy kitchen. I think that's why people stay on my staff, and it means that I can devote my energies to creating new dishes rather than training a sous chef every year," says the 38-year-old native of Normandy.

Pierre's peaceful nature is part of his background and training. He is from a farming family, and until age 19 intended to study veterinary medicine. When he moved to Paris to start his apprenticeship, he was five years older than most of his countrymen who become chefs—something he sees as a plus.

"In addition to working, we had to go to school, and some of the kids could hardly read or write or count," Pierre says. "Those were a crucial five years in my life, and I could cope with the pressure of all the work, and had time left to buy cookbooks and practice much more than I could have if I were younger."

After a stint in the army, Pierre was hired in the kitchen of Lucas Carton, the venerable Parisian restaurant founded at the turn of the century. "It was a classic French restaurant, and people like Paul Bocuse, Michel Guerard and the Troisgros brothers all worked there at various times," he recalls. "I was impressed with the freshness of all the ingredients they used, and all the food was prepared *a la minute*, which was the best practice a young chef could have."

After Lucas Carton, Pierre spent time in the kitchens at the Westbury Hotel in London and the Maxim's restaurants in both Paris and Madrid. He moved to Chicago in 1974 to take command of the kitchen at Le Titi de Paris, purchasing the restaurant from its owners in 1978.

"Eleven years ago there were not too many good restaurants in Chicago, and the food the kitchen here had been preparing for two years was not of the quality of the food in France," Pierre says. "I now think that, in general, the city has caught up, and when I go to France—as I do each year—I come back with ideas, but I don't have the feeling anymore that they have all the good food."

While Pierre has been continually lightening the offerings at Le Titi de Paris ("I still make cassoulet and bouillabaisse a few times a year," he confesses, "but we're not going back to hearty dishes."), its physical setting has remained much the same. A simple country room with tapestry-covered walls above paneling of dark wood, the restaurant features casual arrangements of flowers on the tables and a small bar at the far end of the almost-square, seventy-five-seat dining room, which serves as a holding area.

One of the hallmarks of the restaurant is the way Pierre deftly combines different

meats and fish in the same entrée. He will pair chicken with rack of lamb, and creates a favorite dish by boning a saddle of lamb, and rolling the famous French cut of meat around a veal mousse with a tenderloin of beef in the center.

"You get so much complexity by combining meats or fish or serving the different animals together," he says.

Presentation also is very important to Pierre, and with good reason. "Our customers come here often, and I want them to know they can always find something new and different." ✗

LE TITI DE PARIS
PALATINE

MENU

SAUSAGE OF SPINACH NOODLE
Pasta roll filled with seafood mousse, served with vinegar basil butter sauce

SADDLE OF LAMB WITH FILET OF BEEF
An impressively meaty entrée served with garlic sauce

PROGRÈS WITH TWO CHOCOLATE MOUSSES
An almond-meringue French layer cake topped with mousses of dark and white chocolate

PEAR SOUFFLÉ
A sweet, airy soufflé featuring fresh poached pears

✗

SERVINGS: 12-14
PREPARATION TIME: 45 MINUTES

SAUSAGE OF SPINACH NOODLE

MOUSSE OF PIKE AND SHRIMP
  7 ounces fresh pike fillet, chopped (salmon, redfish, bass or red snapper may be substituted)
  17 ounces fresh shrimp, peeled, deveined and lightly chopped (approximately 2 pounds medium-sized whole fresh shrimp)
  1½ teaspoons salt
  dash of pepper
   1 egg
  1½ cups whipping cream

Place pike and 7 ounces of the shrimp (reserving 10 ounces) into a food processor with the salt, pepper and egg. Purée until creamy. Then, with the processor running, slowly add the cream. Reserve mousse in the refrigerator.

Note: If a meat grinder is available, grind the pike and shrimp before adding to the food processor to save wear on the processor.

PASTA DOUGH

3 ounces fresh spinach
7 ounces flour
2 egg yolks
1 whole egg
¼ teaspoon salt
dash of pepper
½ teaspoon olive oil

Blanch spinach in salted boiling water for 15 seconds. Refresh in ice water. Strain; then squeeze the spinach as dry as possible. With a little of the flour, finely chop the spinach in a food processor; then add remaining flour, egg yolks, whole egg, salt, pepper and olive oil.

Mix until ball of dough forms. Remove the dough from the processor; sprinkle with flour and let rest for 15 to 20 minutes.

On a floured board, roll the dough into 2 rectangles approximately 8-by-14 inches. Cover each rectangle with the prepared mousse and sprinkle with the remaining 10 ounces of shrimp. Roll the sheets of pasta into 14-inch long sausage-shaped rolls. Wrap the rolls in cheesecloth and tie the ends with white string. Tie loosely in the middle 3 or 4 times to keep the sausage shape while cooking. Simmer in salted water, turning occasionally, for 20 minutes. Let rest until ready to remove cheesecloth and serve.

VINEGAR BASIL BUTTER SAUCE

2 tablespoons shallots, chopped
9 ounces cold unsalted butter
½ cup red wine vinegar
1 cup dry white wine
½ cup whipping cream
1 medium tomato, peeled, seeded
    and diced
8 fresh basil leaves, chopped
salt and pepper to taste

Sauté the shallots in 1 teaspoon of the butter until blonde in color. Add the vinegar and reduce until almost dry. Add the white wine and reduce again to very little liquid. Add the cream and bring to a boil. Lower heat to medium and add tomato, salt and pepper. Bit by bit, whisk in the remaining cold butter. Remove from heat, keeping warm. Just before serving, add basil leaves.

LEEK GARNISH

2 medium leeks, green part only,
    julienned
2 teaspoons butter
salt to taste

Sauté the leeks in butter for 5 minutes. Season with salt. Keep warm until use.

Unwrap and slice the pasta roll. Spoon the sauce onto individual serving plates and top with slices of pasta roll. Garnish with sautéed leeks. Sprinkle with chopped chives or parsley if desired.

Saddle of Lamb with Filet of Beef

SADDLE OF LAMB WITH FILET OF BEEF

SERVINGS: 8
PREPARATION TIME: 1½ HOURS

VEAL MOUSSE
½ *pound veal, chopped*
1 *ounce parsley*
1 *egg*
1 *cup whipping cream*
salt and pepper to taste

In a food processor, purée the veal with the parsley, egg, salt and pepper. With the machine running, slowly add the cream. Reserve in the refrigerator.

Note: If a meat grinder is available, grind the veal and parsley before adding to the food processor to save wear on the processor.

SADDLE OF LAMB
1 *whole saddle of lamb, with backbone, approximately 5-7 pounds*
1 *whole beef tenderloin, approximately 2 pounds*
3 *ounces fatback, thinly sliced*
salt and pepper

Trim most of the fat from the inside of the saddle, being careful not to pierce the tenderloin filets on each side of the backbone. Following the bone, remove the 2 tenderloins, leaving them whole. Take out the backbone and reserve for sauce.

Cut out the fat that was underneath the tenderloins and backbone.

(continued)

30

Carefully shave the fat from the outside of the saddle (don't cut into the meat). Trim fat from the tenderloins. With a mallet, pound flat the flap-like flanks of the saddle. Lay the saddle flat skin-side down. Salt and pepper the inside and coat with a layer of half the veal mousse.

Place the lamb tenderloins back in their original position on the saddle. Salt and pepper the beef tenderloin and place in the center of the saddle between the lamb tenderloins. Cover tenderloins with remaining veal mousse. Fold the flanks so that the inside of the saddle is closed. Cover both ends of the rolled saddle with the sliced fatback to keep the mousse inside while roasting. Salt and pepper the outside of the saddle and tie closed with white string approximately 3 times lengthwise and 7 times widthwise. Rub the outside of the saddle with butter and set skin-side up in a roasting pan.

Roast approximately 1 hour in a 400 degree oven to medium rare. Let sit 20 minutes before slicing.

GARLIC SAUCE
bones from saddle of lamb
2 tablespoons butter
1 small onion, chopped
1 small carrot, chopped
½ stalk celery, chopped
2 cloves garlic, chopped
1 small tomato, seeded and chopped
bouquet garni—1 sprig thyme, 1 bay
   leaf and a few parsley stems,
   wrapped in a green leek leaf, tied
   with string
1 teaspoon tomato paste
⅓ cup bourbon
1 cup red wine
3 cups chicken or beef stock
salt and pepper to taste

Using a cleaver, chop the bones into 1-inch pieces. Sauté in butter until well browned. Add the onion, carrot and celery and sauté 5 minutes, until browned. Add garlic, tomato, bouquet garni, tomato paste and bourbon. Briefly reduce; then add red wine. Season with salt and pepper. Reduce to ⅓ cup liquid. Add stock and simmer approximately 35 minutes to approximately 2 cups liquid. Strain before serving.

GARLIC GARNISH
24 garlic cloves
 1 tablespoon butter
½ teaspoon powdered sugar

Blanch garlic for 10 seconds in boiling water. Strain and blanch again in fresh boiling water. Blanch a third time in the same manner. Sauté the blanched garlic in butter and add the powdered sugar.

Remove the strings from the saddle. Serve slices of the saddle with the garlic sauce, garnished with the sautéed garlic cloves.

PROGRÈS LAYER
  3 ounces almonds
  ⅓ ounce flour
  4 ounces sugar
  3 egg whites

Spread almonds on a baking sheet
and toast in a 350 degree oven for 5
to 10 minutes (watching carefully to
avoid burning). Cool at room temperature. Blend in a food processor with
the flour until a powder forms.

   Combine the almond powder and 3
ounces sugar. Set aside. Beat the egg
whites to soft peaks. Slowly add the
remaining ounce of sugar and beat
until stiff peaks are formed. Carefully
fold the dry ingredients into the egg
whites. Pour the batter into an 11-
inch springform pan lined with
parchment paper. Bake at 350 degrees for 15 minutes. Let cool
completely.

DARK CHOCOLATE MOUSSE
  *7 ounces bittersweet chocolate,
    chopped (slightly sweetened
    chocolate available in specialty
    stores)*
  14 ounces whipping cream

Melt the chocolate with half of the
whipping cream. Let cool. Whip the
remaining cream until stiff and fold
into the cooled chocolate. Spread the
dark chocolate mousse on the progrès
layer. Refrigerate about 30 minutes
while preparing the white chocolate
mousse.

WHITE CHOCOLATE MOUSSE
  *9 ounces good quality white
    chocolate, chopped*
  12 ounces whipping cream

Melt chocolate with 5 ounces of the
whipping cream. Cool to room temperature. Beat the remaining cream
until stiff; carefully fold into the
cooled chocolate. Spread on top of
the dark chocolate mousse and return
cake to the refrigerator for several
hours or overnight.

ASSEMBLY
  3 ounces white chocolate shavings
  *3 ounces bittersweet chocolate
    shavings*

Unmold the cake and garnish the top
with white and bittersweet chocolate
shavings just before serving. Serve
with crème anglaise if desired (recipe
follows).

CRÈME ANGLAISE WITH GRAND
MARNIER
  6 egg yolks
  4½ ounces sugar
  2 tablespoons Grand Marnier
  17 ounces milk

Heat egg yolks, sugar and Grand
Marnier in the top of a double boiler.
Scald the milk and add to the egg
yolk mixture, whisking constantly.
Cook over simmering water until
mixture coats a spoon. Cool before
serving.

2 pounds ripe pears, peeled, cored
 and halved
12½ ounces sugar
 9½ ounces water
 1 teaspoon lemon juice, plus a
 splash for the sugar syrup
 2 teaspoons pear brandy
 6 ounces egg whites
powdered sugar

Simmer pears in 7 ounces sugar, 8 ounces water and 1 teaspoon lemon juice for 10 minutes. Drain pears; discard liquid. When cool, chop 2 pear halves and set aside. Purée the rest of the pears. Cook purée for about 5 minutes over high heat, stirring constantly, to remove excess liquid. Set purée aside.

Combine 3½ ounces sugar, 1½ ounces water, and a splash of lemon juice and heat to 275 degrees on a candy thermometer (hard-ball stage) to form sugar syrup. Pour the hot syrup into the pear purée and mix well. Add pear brandy to the purée and let mixure cool. Beat the egg whites on high speed until they begin to hold a shape. Add 2 ounces of sugar and beat until very stiff. Lighten the pear mixture by whisking in 2 tablespoons of the stiff egg whites and then fold in the remaining egg whites. Butter and sugar 6 approximately 4-inch (1 cup) soufflé molds. Fill molds halfway with batter. Sprinkle with half of the reserved chopped pear. Fill molds to the top with batter; then sprinkle with the remaining chopped pear. Tamp molds and clean rims. Bake at 375 degrees for 10 to 15 minutes. Sprinkle soufflés with powdered sugar and serve immediately.

FERNAND GUTIERREZ
THE DINING ROOM

While elegant dining has been part of the French hotel tradition for centuries, calling something "hotel food" in the United States was considered an insult until the past few decades. The elevation of hotel dining is a result, to a large extent, of the creativity and talents of chefs like Fernand Gutierrez, executive chef for the Ritz-Carlton Hotel and its elegant Dining Room.

Fernand has been trained at some of the best hotels in Europe, and chose to remain within the hotel system, where he can command a staff of more than 100 and a budget which allows him to select only the best ingredients.

"I'm big, and I need some space to move around in," says the 34-year-old Dijon native. "I like to see the different operations in the hotel going on at the same time. When we can do perfectly roasted squab at a banquet for 500, at the same time 100 in the Dining Room are having entrées prepared *à la minute*, then I feel a great sense of satisfaction."

Against his parents' wishes, Fernand began his apprenticeship at the Hôtel du Strad at age 14. Three years later, he moved to Grenoble during the 1968 Winter Olympics and worked for renowned chef Roger Verge. His next job was at the Hôtel de Paris in Monte Carlo, and twelve years ago he began working in a series of kitchens in the Bahamas.

He moved to the United States to become chef of the Gourmet Room at the Fairmont Hotel in Atlanta, and was hired for the first time by Chicago's Ritz-Carlton in 1978. He left for a brief tenure as executive sous chef at the Resorts International Hotel in Atlantic City and as executive chef of the Park Plaza Hotel in Boston. Fernand rejoined the Four Seasons Hotel chain—which owns the Ritz-Carlton—to become executive chef of Houston's Inn on the Park when it opened, returning to Chicago in 1983.

"I love Chicago as a city, and there is a sense of competition between the restaurants here that keeps a chef moving forward. We are all going after the same diners, and a hotel restaurant depends on locals as much as any other restaurant," he says.

The Dining Room, his showplace restaurant, is a stately high-ceilinged room which opens onto a skylighted garden. Huge crystal chandeliers softly light the space, with peach and pale blue used as accent colors for the floral latticework carpeting and table linens. A central island is used for the presentation of his pâtés and terrines.

"In the hotel tradition, presentation has always been very important, but even with the size of my staff, we don't have the people needed to serve from silver trays or carve roasts on carts; so, displaying it and making each individual plate a work of art has taken over."

Watching these details is part of Fernand's job. As executive chef, with responsibility for The Dining Room, the less formal Café, the banquet facilities and room service, he has little time to actually get behind a stove, although he does cook for special parties.

"I know food and how tastes go together," he says, "and I'll create a dish on paper, then turn it over to a sous chef to actually cook. But when he brings me the dish and it's good, I get as excited as if I'd cooked it myself."

Some of the dishes are lightened versions of hearty French regional food, but served more elegantly and befitting the environment. A hearty quail dish, for example, is wrapped in a pouch made from a light omelet, an approach similar to a crêpe but more exciting. In the same way, Fernand offers a layered lamb cake based on a traditional recipe from the South of France.

"But basics remain basics, and the trend to lightness has boundaries," he says cautiously. "There is an image to the Ritz, and the food must fit." ✗

THE DINING ROOM
CHICAGO

MENU

SALMON AND SEA BASS TERRINE
The French version of sushi featuring marinated salmon and sea bass

QUAIL IN AN OMELET POUCH
Small roast quails encased in an omelet, tied with strings of leek

TARTELETTE MIKADO
The chef's creation—salsify purée in a small pastry shell, garnished with sliced carrots and truffles

LAYERED LAMB CAKE
A provincial dish made with olive oil, garlic, tomatoes and other ingredients typical in the south of France

WARM APPLE TART
A quick light dessert using puff pastry and apples

⚐

SERVINGS: 12
PREPARATION TIME: 30 MINUTES (NOTE ELAPSED TIME)

SALMON AND SEA BASS TERRINE

TERRINE
1½ pounds salmon fillet, thinly sliced
1½ pounds sea bass fillet, thinly sliced
1 ounce sugar and one ounce salt, combined
juice of 1 lemon
2 ounces dry white wine

Line a 3-pound terrine with waxed paper. Alternate layers of salmon and sea bass, sprinkling each layer with the sugar and salt mixture, lemon juice and white wine until the mold is full. Cover the top with wax paper. Tip the mold and drain any excess liquid. Weight the top with a large juice or vegetable can and marinate in the refrigerator for 3 days.

DRESSING
 3 ounces ginger, peeled and chopped
18 ounces salad oil
 6 ounces lemon juice
½ ounce chervil, chopped
½ ounce parsley, chopped
½ ounce chives, chopped

Marinate ginger in salad oil and
lemon juice. Refrigerate for 3 days.
Just before serving, put the ginger
and marinade in a blender and blend
for three seconds. Add the herbs and
pulse the blender just once to incorporate (don't blend too much or the
dressing will turn white). Reserve.

Unmold the terrine and slice into
individual servings (an electric knife
works well since the terrine is very
delicate). Place the terrine slices on
chilled plates. Serve with the
dressing.

SERVINGS: 4
PREPARATION TIME: 1 HOUR

QUAIL IN AN OMELET
POUCH

QUAIL AND SAUCE
 4 boned quails, 3 ounces each
 6 ounces goose liver mousse
½ ounce salad oil
 4 slices bacon
 1 carrot, diced
 2 stalks celery, diced
 1 small onion, diced
 1 bay leaf
 1 sprig thyme
 2 ounces port
4-8 ounces veal demi-glace (see
   page 99)
½ ounce semi-soft unsalted butter
salt and pepper

Slice each quail open through the
back, leaving the breast whole. Bone
quails and then place skin-side down
on a flat surface, extending them as
far as possible. Season lightly with
salt and pepper. Place one-fourth of
the goose liver mousse onto the center of each quail. Wrap the outer
edges of the quail over the mousse,
overlapping where necessary, so that
the mousse is totally enclosed. Wrap
a slice of bacon around each quail to
hold it together. Secure each with a
piece of white string. Heat an ovenproof sauté pan and add the oil.
Place the quails in the pan, skin-side
up, to brown. Add the diced vegetables, bay leaf, and thyme. Turn the
quails and brown the other side.
Then turn again so that the skin-side
faces up. Place the pan in a preheated 375 degree oven until the
quails are just hot inside, approximately 15 minutes. Take the quails
out of the oven. Remove them from
the roasting pan and reserve in a
warm place.

(continued)

Sauté the diced vegetables and herbs. Drain off fat. Deglaze the pan with the port and reduce the liquid by half. Add the demi-glace. Bring the sauce to a boil and then reduce heat to simmer for about 5 minutes. When the sauce reaches the desired consistency, strain it into a small saucepan. Just before serving, add the butter to the sauce and incorporate it by agitating the pan. Correct seasoning. Reserve, keeping warm.

OMELETS
4 eggs
1 teaspoon water
scant amount of oil
salt and pepper to taste

Beat the eggs, salt and pepper. Add the water. Heat and brush a non-stick 10-inch pan lightly with oil. Pour ¼ of the batter into the pan. Rapidly turn the pan back and forth to create a thin even coat of batter (as for a crêpe). Cook over high heat for 2 to 3 minutes until golden brown. Do not turn the omelet. Carefully remove the omelet from the pan and set aside; make a total of 4 omelets.

LEEK STRINGS
2 large leek leaves (scallions or chives may be substituted)

Blanch the leek leaves in boiling water until soft but not mushy, about 3 minutes. Immediately refresh in ice water. Cut two ½-inch strips lengthwise down each leaf. Set aside.

ASSEMBLY
Remove the string from the quails. Remove the bacon (optional). Place one quail on the center of each omelet (with browned side of the omelet facing down). Gather the edges of the omelet together, to enclose the quail, and tie the omelet one inch from the top with the leek strings. To warm, place the pouches in the oven briefly. Spoon sauce onto four serving plates and place one quail in the center of each.

Tartelette Mikado

SERVINGS: 4
PREPARATION TIME: 1 HOUR

SALSIFY PURÉE

*12 ounces salsify (4-5 whole), peeled
   and rough chopped (turnips may
   be substituted)*
½ quart milk
1 tablespoon butter
2 tablespoons heavy cream
salt and pepper

Cover and cook the salsify in slightly
salted milk for 20 minutes, until
tender. Drain off the milk; purée the
salsify. Pass purée through a fine
sieve into a small saucepan and add
butter and heavy cream while stirring over medium heat. Season to
taste. Reserve, keeping warm.

SAUCE

1 carrot, diced
2 celery stalks, diced
1 small onion, diced
1 shallot, chopped
1 tablespoon salad oil
1 bay leaf
1 sprig thyme
1 ounce Madeira
*4-8 ounces veal demi-glace (see
   page 99)*
1 tablespoon semi-soft unsalted butter

Brown the vegetables in the oil. Add
the bay leaf and thyme. Deglaze with
Madeira and reduce to half. Add the
demi-glace and reduce again by half

(continued)

at a simmer, about 3 minutes. Strain sauce and add butter. Agitate pan to incorporate. Reserve, keeping warm.

ASSEMBLY
6 ounces carrots, blanched and sliced
  1/8-inch thick
4 large truffles, thinly sliced
2 tablespoons clarified butter
8 small tartelette (pie crust) shells,
  precooked (frozen or from recipe on
  page 83, omitting sugar)

Briefly warm the carrots and truffles in the clarified butter. Put the salsify purée in a pastry bag and pipe into the tartelette shells, completely covering the bottom. Place sliced carrots on top of the salsify in half of the shells and arrange sliced truffles on top of the salsify in the other half. Serve each person one carrot and one truffle tartelette, surrounded by sauce.

LAYERED LAMB CAKE

SERVINGS: 4
PREPARATION TIME: 1 HOUR

LAMB AND SAUCE
2 racks of lamb, 1 3/4-2 pounds each
2 sprigs thyme
1 carrot, diced
1 celery stalk, diced
1 small onion, diced
1 bay leaf
4-8 ounces veal demi-glace (see page
  99)
1 ounce olive oil
1 ounce semi-soft unsalted butter
salt and pepper to taste

Completely trim the loins from both racks of lamb, reserving bones and fat. Press the leaves of 1 sprig of thyme on the loins and set aside. Sauté the lamb bones in the reserved fat until browned. Add the diced vegetables, remaining thyme, and bay leaf. When all the ingredients are well browned, add the demi-glace and simmer about 3 minutes. Strain sauce and incorporate butter by agitating pan. Season and reserve, keeping warm. In an ovenproof sauté pan, heat the olive oil until very hot. Season the lamb loins with salt and pepper and sear them in the hot oil

until brown on all sides. Place in a 375 degree oven for about 15 minutes, until rare or medium rare according to preference. Just before assembly, slice into 1/8-thick slices.

TOMATO GARNISH
1/2 shallot, minced
 1 clove garlic, minced
1/2 ounce olive oil
1/2 small onion, diced
 3 large tomatoes, seeded and diced
 1 ounce white wine
pinch of thyme
dash of sugar
1/2 teaspoon tomato paste (only if
  tomatoes are not fully ripe)
pinch of basil
salt and pepper to taste

Cook shallot and garlic in hot oil until tender. Add the onion and tomatoes and toss together. Add the wine, thyme, salt and pepper, and sugar. Add the tomato paste if necessary. Cook until almost dry (cooking time depends on juiciness of tomatoes). Remove from heat. Just before assembly, add the basil.

SPINACH GARNISH

½ shallot, minced
¼ ounce garlic, minced
dash of olive oil
12 ounces spinach, blanched
salt and pepper to taste

Cook shallot and garlic in olive oil until tender. Add spinach and toss. Salt and pepper to taste. Keep warm.

MUSHROOM GARNISH

½ shallot, minced
¼ ounce garlic, minced
dash of olive oil
4 ounces mushrooms, sliced
salt and pepper to taste

Cook shallot and garlic in olive oil until tender. Add mushrooms and sauté. Season with salt and pepper. Keep warm.

ASSEMBLY

Build a layered "cake" on each serving plate using a 5-inch ring as a mold (a five pound coffee can cut at 1½-inch intervals works well). Fill the bottom of the mold with a layer of one-fourth of the spinach, lightly pressing it flat. Form a second layer in the same manner with one-fourth of the mushroom mixture. Top with one-fourth of the tomato mixture. Starting from the center of each cake, place one-fourth of the slices of lamb in a spiral, overlapping each slice as you go. Remove the ring and repeat with each of the remaining three serving plates.

Spoon sauce around the base of each cake. Garnish with thyme and seeded, diced tomatoes if desired.

SERVINGS: 12
PREPARATION TIME: 15 MINUTES

WARM APPLE TART

18 ounces puff pastry (purchase frozen and thaw according to instructions on package)
10-12 apples, peeled, cored and very thinly sliced
3 ounces powdered sugar

On a floured surface, roll out the puff pastry to form a very thin sheet. Cut 12 6-inch circles and prick them with a fork. Place the circles of pastry onto baking sheets covered with parchment paper. Arrange the apple slices on the circles in a spiral pattern. Bake in a preheated 400 degree oven for 10 minutes, or until pastry is brown around the edges. Take pastry out of the oven and sprinkle with powdered sugar. Bake an additional minute. Serve one apple tart per person. Serve with whipped cream on the side if desired.

JOHN DRAZ
THE WINNETKA GRILL

John Draz, the 23-year-old chef of the Winnetka Grill, is part of the new breed of American chef who never felt they had to apologize for American food, believe American food is not a fad but here to stay and delight in basing dishes on the nuances of American regions the way generations of French chefs drew inspiration from the culinary divisions of that country.

"I don't feel Americans should feel inferior in any aspects of the arts," John says, "and while I love the flavors of New Orleans, the Southwest, the foods of New England and the Pacific Northwest, I think the Midwest has been passed over and it is full of all kinds of beautiful food. I love working with the veal and cheeses from Wisconsin and the corn-fed beef in the Midwest cannot be beaten."

Like many of his contemporaries, including Lawrence Forgione at An American Place in New York and Marcel Desaulniers at The Trellis in Williamsburg, Virginia, John developed this attitude while studying at the Culinary Institute of America in Hyde Park, New York. He maintained it while receiving additional training in French techniques that he deftly applies to American ingredients.

When Henry Markwood and John Stoltzman, owners of the Winnetka Grill, hired Draz—then a sous chef at the Ritz-Carlton Hotel—both the style of food and the environment in which it was served changed for him.

The ninety-seat restaurant, located on Chicago's North Shore, features a stark but warm post-modern interior. The entry area is marked by a geometric mosaic of colored woods in the floor, and geometric columns with gilt balls as capitals define the space. The walls are painted with subtle murals of clouds, and the dusty turquoise banquettes are separated with canvas panels looped with rope through large metal circles.

In high school, John was a voracious reader on the subject of food and attended cooking courses in a nearby suburb. "I knew that was what I wanted to do," he says. "I was making extra money as a banquet waiter in various hotels around town, so, I applied for the union's scholarship to the Culinary Institute and got it."

He terms his Culinary Institute training as "broad education, with everything from table service to wine and spirits as part of it," but considers Edward Merard, chef of the Ritz-Carlton where he went to work after graduation in 1981, his first mentor.

"He was strict and from the old school, but I learned the importance of organization. He used to say, 'Any idiot can cook, but wait until you have to start thinking for forty or fifty people!'"

His second mentor was Phillip Stocks, chef at the Café Provençal, whom he credits with "getting my creative juices going." Stocks often would walk into the refrigerator, see what foods were available, and tell John to come up with his own creations.

Most of the food at the restaurant is grilled, over a combination of hardwood charcoal and mesquite chips for additional aroma and flavor. And John believes the foods placed on the grill are the centerpiece of his dishes.

"The entrée item should be the star of the plate, and the sauces and any garnishes are subordinate to it," he says. A veal chop, for example, is grilled to a perfect medium rare, and then complemented by a stock reduction sauce made with Port wine. Or he grills a loin of pork and serves it with apple and cornbread stuffing, a Southern traditional favorite he has lightened.

"Part of the freedom of American cooking is letting yourself go if you have a good sense of what goes well together," John says. "When I combine ingredients they may seem strange in a recipe, but what I am after is the flavor of the finished dish." ✕

THE WINNETKA GRILL
WINNETKA

MENU

GRILLED OYSTERS WITH SMOKED HAM AND FRIED PARSLEY
Oysters on the half shell, served with a tasty parsley garnish

BUTTERNUT SQUASH RAVIOLI WITH CREAM AND ASIAGO CHEESE
A rich appetizer distinguished by sweet squash and a piquant cheese sauce

MESQUITE ROAST LOIN OF PORK WITH APPLE AND CORNBREAD STUFFING
Pork with a Midwestern touch and a panoply of regional ingredients

CHOCOLATE AND BOURBON PECAN CAKE
A flourless chocolate cake with the lingering flavor of bourbon

𓀈

SERVINGS: 4
PREPARATION TIME: 30 MINUTES

GRILLED OYSTERS WITH SMOKED HAM AND FRIED PARSLEY

12 oysters
8 ounces soft unsalted butter
2 medium shallots, minced
2 tablespoons parsley, chopped
juice of ½ lemon
1 tablespoon fennel seed, cracked
2 ounces smoked ham, diced
2 bunches fresh parsley
oil for deep frying
1 lemon for garnish
salt and white pepper to taste

Scrub and open oysters, leaving them on the half shell. Rinse oysters if desired. Set aside. In a mixing bowl whip together butter, shallots, chopped parsley, lemon juice and fennel seed to make compound butter. Season to taste with salt and white pepper. Top each oyster with a pinch of smoked ham and a dollop of compound butter according to the size of the oyster. Place oysters on a barbecue grill with a lid, over a hot fire. Cover and cook until butter is bubbling and oysters start to curl at the edge, about 3 to 4 minutes (depending on the heat). Cut the longer, thicker parts of the stem off the 2 bunches of parsley. Thoroughly wash and dry the parsley; fry in a deep-fat fryer at 350 degrees for 30 seconds or until crisp. Drain and place on a towel to absorb the excess oil. Season with salt and white pepper.

Place a bed of fried parsley on each serving plate. Arrange 3 oysters per plate on the parsley. Garnish each place with a half lemon crown.

Grilled Oysters with Smoked Ham and Fried Parsley

SERVINGS: 4-6
PREPARATION TIME: 1 HOUR

SQUASH FILLING
1 medium butternut squash
pinch of nutmeg
salt and white pepper to taste

Pare and seed the squash. Dice into small cubes. Steam until tender, about 10 to 12 minutes. Place steamed squash in a food processor and purée. Season with nutmeg, salt and white pepper. Remove from processor and cool.

SAUCE
2½ cups heavy cream
½ cup Asiago cheese, grated
salt and white pepper to taste

In a shallow pan, simmer the cream and reduce to two-thirds the volume. Stir in the grated cheese and simmer to melt. Adjust the seasoning and reserve, keeping warm.

BUTTERNUT SQUASH
RAVIOLI WITH CREAM
AND ASIAGO CHEESE

PASTA

  2 cups all-purpose flour
  1 cup semolina flour
  3 eggs
1½ ounces water
  1 tablespoon salt
  1 egg, beaten (egg wash)

Mix together all ingredients except the egg. Knead for approximately 5 minutes. Cover dough and let stand 5 minutes. Using a crank-type pasta machine on the thinnest setting, roll out 6 evenly-trimmed, 12-inch long sheets of pasta. On a floured board, brush one sheet of pasta with the beaten egg. Place 4 spoonfuls of squash ½ inch from the near edge, about 1-inch apart, along the length of the pasta sheet. Fold the far edge of the pasta over the filling so that it meets the near edge. Lightly press the top and bottom layers between the pockets of filling to force out any excess air. Using a fluted ravioli wheel, cut and seal the ravioli by running the wheel between the pockets and along the sides. (If ravioli wheel is unavailable, a fork and knife will work.) Repeat with the remaining pasta sheets.

Plunge ravioli into a large pot of salted boiling water. Cook al dente, about 2 minutes. Remove ravioli from the pot with a slotted spoon and toss in the sauce until well coated.

Serve 4 to 6 ravioli topped with sauce per person. Garnish with Asiago cheese and, if desired, chopped parsley.

MESQUITE ROAST LOIN OF PORK WITH APPLE AND CORNBREAD STUFFING

SERVINGS: 4
PREPARATION TIME: 2 HOURS (NOTE ELAPSED TIME)

ROAST LOIN OF PORK AND STUFFING

1 boneless closely-trimmed pork loin, 2½-3 pounds
1 tart apple, peeled, cored and finely diced
6 ounces ground pork
3 cups cornbread, crumbled
1 cup apple cider
2 tablespoons parsley, chopped
pinch of rosemary
pinch of thyme
salt and white pepper to taste

Insert a knife through the length of the loin making a 2-inch slit. Set loin aside. Combine remaining ingredients in a mixing bowl to make stuffing. Be sure there are no large lumps of ground pork or cornbread. If the stuffing seems too dry, add more cider. Put stuffing into a pastry bag with an opening large enough to allow the apple to pass through. Pipe the stuffing into both ends of the cavity cut into the loin. Season the outside of the loin with salt and black pepper. Place on a barbecue grill with lid over a low fire fueled with hardwood charcoal and water-soaked mesquite chips. Cover and roast slowly, turning frequently until internal temperature reaches 150 degrees, approximately 1½ hours. Or, bake in a covered roasting pan in a 325 to 350 degree oven for approximately 1½ hours.

Allow loin to rest 20 minutes before carving.

SAUCE
½ ounce unsalted butter
2 tablespoons shallots, chopped
1 cup cider
2 cups veal demi-glace (see recipe page 99)
1 ounce apple brandy

Melt butter in a saucepan and sauté shallots until soft. Deglaze with apple cider and reduce liquid by one-half. Add demi-glace and simmer 5 minutes, skimming any foam that rises to the surface. Away from the stove, add the apple brandy to the sauce. Bring back to a boil. Remove from heat; adjust seasoning and strain. To serve, place slices of pork loin on individual serving plates and spoon sauce around.

Note: Leftover stuffing can be baked in an overproof dish and served with the roast loin of pork.

SERVINGS: 12
PREPARATION TIME: 2 HOURS (NOTE ELAPSED TIME)

CHOCOLATE BOURBON AND PECAN CAKE

12 ounces semi-sweet chocolate, chopped
8 ounces unsalted butter
8 eggs
1½ cups sugar
½ cup bourbon
1 pound pecans, finely ground just before use

GLAZE
1 pound semi-sweet chocolate, chopped
⅓ cup vegetable oil

Melt chocolate in double boiler. Stir in vegetable oil. Reserve.

ASSEMBLY
18 large pecan halves

Butter the bottom and sides of a 12-inch springform pan. Place buttered parchment paper on the bottom of the pan and dust bottom and sides with sugar. Melt the chocolate in a double boiler. Cut butter into small pieces and stir into the chocolate until melted. Set aside and keep warm. Separate the eggs. Whip the egg whites until foamy. Add half the sugar and continue whipping until the egg whites are stiff. Set aside. Whip the remaining sugar and the egg yolks until ribbony. Mix in the melted chocolate and bourbon. Alternately fold in the ground pecans and egg whites. Pour the batter into the prepared springform pan and bake in a preheated 300 degree oven for 1½ to 1¾ hours. Remove from the oven and cool.

Remove cake from springform pan and place on icing rack, inverted. Ladle glaze over cake and spread to cover top and sides. Garnish by placing pecan halves around the top rim. Refrigerate cake for 30 minutes to allow glaze to harden before serving.

BERNARD CRETIER
LE VICHYSSOIS

Diners in France are never deterred by driving an hour for a meal of superb caliber, and the success of Bernard Cretier's Le Vichyssois, located in the village of Lakemoor about 50 miles northwest of Chicago, proves that Americans share this spirit.

It's not that the 38-year-old native of Vichy purposely selected a location for his seventy-seat restaurant, which he opened in 1976, about equidistant between Chicago and Milwaukee. But when he was prepared to realize his dream of commanding a kitchen in a restaurant he owned, the white brick-and-wooden building was the only one he could afford.

"I wanted to be a free spirit and didn't want any partners, and, the price was right although the location was not," Bernard recalls. "I had to hope my customers from Chicago would make the trip, and what I didn't know was that Le Vichyssois would become the meeting place when friends from Chicago and Milwaukee wanted to get together for dinner."

The pale gray and taupe interior, with its rustic wooden touches and copper pots and porcelain plates decorating the walls, complements the classic food Bernard produces in the kitchen. The same sense of "free spirit" that brought him to Lakemoor controls his creative impulses: He doesn't cook a dish if he doesn't like it, even if it might please some customers.

Bernard cemented his philosophy of individualism while working for two of the greatest combined talents in France, Jean and Pierre Troisgros.

"I knew I wanted to become a chef when I was 13 years old, and my parents thought I was nuts," he says. "So during one summer when I was 15, instead of sending me to England, as they often did, they arranged for me to work for the Troisgros. They thought I would get disgusted and go back to school happily, and I didn't leave for three years."

He was then hired by Paul Bocuse for his restaurant near Lyons, which was followed by two years in the army as a chef for the French Secretary of State. After the army, Bernard worked in restaurants in France, Germany and Switzerland, finally settling at famed Maxim's in Paris for three years, after which he was transferred to Maxim's in Chicago as a sous chef.

Bernard developed his own style of cooking, far simpler than the one at Maxim's, and used to try out dishes once a month for a group of friends. "If they liked it, I would save the idea. I knew then that I wanted my own restaurant," he says.

"I'm not fancy, and I don't believe in fancy food," Bernard says, "but I try to stay close to whatever dish I prepare. I don't like overpowering sauces, but I do like to pair sauces on a dish that complement each other."

One dish that has become a trademark of the restaurant is seafood pâté, always served hot and topped with a light tomato and basil sauce. Although the combination of fish can vary from week to week, the presentation does not. "It melts in your mouth when it's hot," he says of the pâté, "and I can't believe people serve it cold. It tastes mushy and not appealing to me that way."

Much of Bernard's creative efforts go into the long list of nightly specials, as many as twelve to fourteen on a given evening. The menu changes seasonally, with game—including venison—emphasized during the winter. One dish that will stay on the menu despite the season is a sinfully rich Tarte au Chocolate, a dense cake with the texture and intensity of flavor of fudge.

"I have customers who order dessert before they've even had an appetizer," Bernard says, "and if they come all this way I certainly want to please them." ✗

LE VICHYSSOIS
LAKEMOOR

MENU

SEAFOOD PÂTÉ IN BASIL SAUCE
A delicate terrine featuring walleye pike, salmon and shrimp, served with a tomato basil sauce

SALMON BAKED IN PUFF PASTRY
Norwegian salmon fillets filled with salmon mousse, wrapped in puff pastry, and served with sauce champagne

TARTE AU CHOCOLAT
A frosted chocolate layer cake, served with cranberry sauce

𝑥

SERVINGS: 10
PREPARATION TIME: 2 ½ HOURS

SEAFOOD PÂTÉ IN A BASIL SAUCE

SEAFOOD MOUSSE
  1 pound walleye pike fillet (brook trout fillet or peeled, deveined shrimp may be substituted)
  3 eggs
  28 ounces whipping cream
  2 ounces salmon fillet, diced
  2 ounces shrimp, peeled, deveined, and diced
  2-3 tablespoons parsley, chopped
  salt and pepper to taste

Chill blade and bowl of food processor in freezer for 5 to 10 minutes.
  Purée 14 ounces of the walleye pike in a food processor. Add salt, pepper and eggs. With machine running, slowly add cream. Correct sea-soning to taste. Pour the mousse into a bowl. Dice the remaining 2 ounces of pike. Add the diced pike, salmon and shrimp to the mousse. Add the parsley and stir until well blended. Pour the mousse into a well-buttered ovenproof 9-by-5-by-3 inch dish. Tamp dish against counter to remove any trapped air bubbles. Cover top of dish with waxed paper, then with aluminum foil. Place in a larger pan filled with about 2 inches of hot water. Bake in a 375 degree oven for 1 to 1½ hours, until a knife inserted into the pâté comes out hot and clean. Set aside in a warm place for 15 minutes before slicing.

BASIL SAUCE

2-3 tablespoons olive oil
 1 clove garlic, peeled and chopped
    into 3 pieces
½ medium onion, chopped
 2 teaspoons basil
24 ounces tomato juice
 2 tablespoons parsley, chopped
salt and pepper to taste

Put the olive oil in a large saucepan. Add the garlic, onion and basil and cook slowly over low heat for about 5 minutes until onions are tender but not brown. Add tomato juice. Adjust seasoning with salt and pepper and bring to a boil. Reduce heat and simmer 10 to 15 minutes. Just before serving, remove garlic and add parsley.

Remove wax paper and aluminum foil from the top of the pâté. Invert and unmold on a plate. Slice pâté with an electric knife (because pâté is very fragile). To serve, spoon basil sauce around slices of pâté on each plate.

SERVINGS: 8
PREPARATION TIME: 2 HOURS (NOTE ELAPSED TIME)

SALMON BAKED IN PUFF PASTRY

SALMON MOUSSE

 6 ounces salmon fillet (Norwegian
    salmon works best)
 1 egg
12 ounces whipping cream
 8 salmon fillets, 4 ounces each
 8 pieces of puff pastry,
    approximately 5-by-7 inches each
 1 egg, beaten (egg wash)
salt and pepper to taste

Chill blade and bowl of food processor in freezer for 5 to 10 minutes.

Purée the 6 ounces of salmon in a food processor. Add the salt, pepper and egg. With the machine running, slowly add cream. Adjust seasoning. Pour the mousse into a bowl and refrigerate for 1 hour.

Butterfly the 4-ounce salmon fillets so that they have a pocket covered by two flaps. With flaps open, place a generous spoonful of salmon mousse into pockets. Close the flaps over the mousse (they will not completely cover the filling) and set the fillets in the refrigerator for 10 minutes. Season salmon with salt and pepper.

Set each filled salmon on one side of each pastry piece. Brush the edges of the puff pastry with the egg wash; then fold the pastry over the salmon. Pinch the edges of the puff pastry to seal. Brush the top of the packets with egg wash. Refrigerate for 10 minutes. Set the packets, with the longest sealed side toward the middle, on a baking sheet which has been covered with parchment paper. Bake in a preheated 400 to 425 degree oven for 20 minutes until the pastry is golden brown. Reserve in a warm place.

51

SAUCE CHAMPAGNE

½ bottle of dry champagne or
    sparkling wine
4-5 ounces salmon bones (ask your
    butcher for these)
2 medium to large shallots, chopped
24 ounces whipping cream
salt and pepper to taste

Reduce champagne, salmon bones, and shallots over high heat to a glaze, about 20 minutes. Add cream, mix well and reduce until it coats the back of a spoon. Season with salt and pepper to taste. Strain and reserve in a warm place. With an electric knife, cut the salmon packets into 3 pieces. To serve, spoon champagne sauce around each salmon packet.

TARTE AU CHOCOLAT

SERVINGS: 8-10
PREPARATION TIME: 1½ HOURS

CAKE

3⅓ ounces orange chocolate (semi-
    sweet chocolate may be
    substituted)
3⅓ ounces butter
1⅔ ounces flour
5 ounces sugar
3 eggs

In the top of a double boiler, melt chocolate. Add butter, whisking to melt and incorporate. In a separate bowl, beat flour, sugar and eggs with mixer for about 3 minutes, until smooth and creamy. Add the melted chocolate and butter. Pour into an 8-inch round pan, that has been buttered and lightly floured. Bake in a 375 degree oven for 20 minutes until a toothpick comes out clean. Let cool completely before frosting.

CRANBERRY SAUCE

1 cup orange juice
½ cup water
6 ounces whole fresh cranberries
½ cup sugar
zest (pith-free peel) of ½ orange,
    grated

Combine the ingredients in a saucepan and boil for 20 minutes, stirring occasionally. Purée with a food processor. Strain and refrigerate.

Tarte au Chocolat

FROSTING

1½ *ounces orange chocolate*
    (bittersweet chocolate may be
    substituted)
1½ *ounces bittersweet chocolate*
    (slightly sweetened chocolate may
    be found in a specialty store)
 ⅓ *ounce (2 teaspoons) butter*
3⅓ *ounces whipping cream*

In the top of a double boiler, melt the chocolate. Add the butter. Bring the cream to a boil and add to the chocolate. Let cool until thick and creamy.

Spread frosting over the top and sides of the cake. To garnish, sprinkle the top with cocoa powder and powdered sugar. To serve, pour cranberry sauce around slices.

JEAN BANCHET
LE FRANÇAIS

The twinkling dark eyes and smiling face of Jean Banchet beam from the cover of a *Bon Appetit*, proclaiming his Le Français in Wheeling "America's Best Restaurant," a declaration it has not re-awarded since that 1980 edition.

Surrounding the magazine in the small waiting room are honors to support the assertion—a string of Mobil Travel Guide Five-Star awards, a gold plate from Cartier's Fine Dining program and books of press clippings kept up to date by Jean's wife Doris,

who runs the dining room with the speed and efficiency exhibited by her husband and his staff in the kitchen.

While the reputation of Le Français has grown since its opening in 1973 (to the point that diners from around the country make dinner reservations before they book hotels or flights to the city), Jean's own reputation and standards have been spread by the many chefs he has trained now commanding their own kitchens.

The secret? Both the standards for food

and for service are identical to those of the French restaurants in which he was trained. And in the same way that he has not relaxed those standards, he has maintained a climate of discipline in the kitchen—but always with time to teach.

"I scream a lot, and I don't take any excuses if something is not good, but then I take the time to show them exactly how something should be done," says the 44-year-old. "I'm not going to bone a duck myself, but I will taste the seasoning to make sure it becomes a perfect pâté."

Jean's own training, starting at age 13 in the kitchen of La Pyramide, played a part in his meteoric rise. Although the hours were grueling, after two years he had reached the rank of *premier comis*, a station just before *demi-chef*, an unusual accomplishment when still in one's mid-teens.

A fellow apprentice was Paul Bocuse, who became a life-long friend and offered Jean a job at the restaurant he had taken over from his father. What followed was a year at the Hotel de Paris in Monte Carlo, and two years in Algeria where he performed his military service by becoming a chef to General La Roux. At 21, Jean was asked to command the kitchen at the Sporting Club, a casino in the Knightsbridge section of London.

"I knew by the time I went into the army that I was going to make it. After La Pyramide all the doors were open, but London was the big step," he says.

In 1968, he accepted Hugh Hefner's offer to open the Playboy Club's resort at Lake Geneva, Wisconsin. Being an executive chef was far too sedentary a job, so he moved to Chicago and worked for three restaurants before opening his own.

Because many of the dishes were new to American diners, Jean began his trademark—one copied by restaurants run by his former assistants across the country. He does elaborate cart presentations, with each plated and garnished as the plate is for the diner. The cart is then rolled to the table in the elegant dining room, also rivaling any in France.

The dark wood walls are lit by windows curtained in white lace, and enlivened by hanging copper pots, mounted feathered game and a portrait of the chef in one of his rare moments of repose. A rich tapestry in muted tones covers the dark wood chairs and banquettes.

Jean's unbending quest for the finest ingredients and meticulous preparation have remained unaltered since the restaurant first opened. He still buys game birds with the feathers on and cleans them himself; he still imports most of his ingredients from France.

"I am dedicated to showing people what the best can be," he says. "I do mainly traditional food, but the basic food and how it is prepared is the finest you can find anywhere—including in France." ✗

LE FRANÇAIS
WHEELING

MENU

SQUAB SALAD WITH WILD MUSHROOMS AND QUAIL EGGS

Dressed mixed greens with roast breast and leg of squab, five varieties of wild mushrooms, and sautéed quail eggs

LOBSTER WITH NOODLES, BASIL AND CAVIAR

Medallions of steamed lobster with noodles and a tomato cream sauce

ROAST SWEETBREADS WITH BELGIAN ENDIVES AND TRUFFLES

Sweetbreads accompanied by julienned Belgian endives and a truffle cream sauce

NOISETTE OF VENISON WITH GRAND-VENEUR SAUCE

Marinated medallions of venison loin sautéed and served with confit chestnut

RASPBERRY FEUILLETÉ

Baked puff pastry filled with fresh berries and chantilly cream, served with caramel sauce

GRAND MARNIER SOUFFLÉ

An ethereal soufflé made without flour

ϰ

SERVINGS: 4
PREPARATION TIME: 20 MINUTES

2 squabs, 16 ounces each
2 ounces clarified butter
½ pound mixed wild mushrooms (a combination of enoki, oyster, chanterelle, mutton foot and shiitake works well)
1 tablespoon olive oil
1 tablespoon red wine vinegar
16 ounces squab stock (chicken stock may be substituted)
10 ounces chives, chopped
2 ounces red leaf lettuce, chopped

2 ounces curly endive, chopped
2 ounces Belgian endive, chopped
2 ounces lamb's lettuce (mache), chopped
2 ounces Boston lettuce, chopped
2 ounces green beans, blanched and chopped
4 ounces vinaigrette dressing
8 quail eggs
4 leaves Boston lettuce
4 leaves red leaf lettuce
salt and pepper to taste

(continued)

Squab Salad with Wild Mushrooms and Quail Eggs

Bone the squab breast and legs. Season with salt and pepper and sauté in clarified butter in an ovenproof pan for about 1 minute. Cook the squab in a 450 degree oven for about 3 to 4 minutes, until medium rare. Season mushrooms with salt and pepper and sauté in olive oil until tender. Reserve in a warm place.

Remove the breasts and legs from the roasting pan and reserve, keeping warm. Pour off grease. Deglaze the pan with vinegar and reduce about 1 minute. Add the stock and reduce several minutes. Remove from heat. Add the chives. Reserve, keeping warm. Toss the chopped lettuces and green beans with the vinaigrette. Fry the quail eggs "sunnyside up" in a non-stick pan with a scant amount of clarified butter. Arrange a bed of Boston and red lettuces on each serving plate. Top with the dressed chopped lettuce and green beans. Slice the squab and arrange pinwheel fashion on top of the salad. Spoon mushrooms around the salad. Place a fried quail egg on top of the salad on either side. Pour the reduced stock around the salad and serve.

LOBSTER WITH NOODLES, BASIL AND CAVIAR

4 live lobsters, 2 pounds each
2 ounces clarified butter
2 ounces shallots, chopped
1 ounce fresh tarragon (or ½ teaspoon dried)
2 tomatoes, diced
½ cup cognac
½ cup sherry
1 cup white wine
1-1½ quarts heavy cream
1 cup heavily reduced fish stock
2 ounces fresh butter
2 ounces fresh basil, chopped (or ½ teaspoon dried)
1 pound noodles, cooked al dente in boiling salted water
salt and pepper to taste

Steam lobsters for 8 to 10 minutes. Remove the meat from the shell and reserve, keeping warm. Finely chop the lobster shell and place in a heated saucepan with the clarified butter. Sauté for 4 to 5 minutes; then add the shallots, tarragon and tomatoes. Sauté another 5 minutes; then add the cognac, sherry and white wine.

Reduce by two-thirds; add half of the heavy cream and fish stock. Season with salt and pepper. Reduce for 5 minutes; strain; adjust seasoning and reserve, keeping warm. In a sauté pan, combine the remaining cream, fresh butter, basil and salt and pepper and heat about 1 minute. Add the noodles and reduce until cream thickens and coats the noodles. Reserve, keeping warm.

ASSEMBLY
2 tomatoes, peeled, seeded and chopped
scant amount of olive oil
2 ounces Beluga caviar

Salt and pepper the tomatoes to taste. Sauté in olive oil briefly, just to warm. Slice the lobster into medallions and arrange around the rim of each serving plate. Place noodles in the center of the plate. Spoon sauce over the lobster; top with caviar. Garnish the noodles with the sautéed tomatoes and serve.

ROAST SWEETBREADS WITH BELGIAN ENDIVES AND TRUFFLES

2 pounds sweetbreads
juice from 1 lemon
2 tablespoons clarified butter
6 large Belgian endives, julienned
1 quart heavy cream
4 ounces truffles, julienned
1 tablespoon shallot, finely chopped
½ cup vermouth
2 tablespoons chicken glaze (chicken base available in specialty shops may be sustituted)
salt and pepper to taste

Soak sweetbreads in cold water overnight in the refrigerator. Strain sweetbreads and blanch them in fresh water with half of the lemon juice. Strain again and set aside to cool. Heat an ovenproof sauté pan and add 1 tablespoon clarified butter. Season the sweetbreads with salt and pepper and sauté until brown on both sides. Place the pan in a 450 degree oven for 10 minutes.

Season the julienned endives with

(continued)

salt and pepper and sauté in the remaining clarified butter and lemon juice. After about 1 minute, add half the cream to the endives and briefly reduce. Add the julienned truffles and simmer to reduce.

Take the sweetbreads out of the oven and remove from pan, reserving in a warm place. Drain the fat from the pan and add the shallots. Deglaze the pan with vermouth and add the chicken glaze. Reduce for 1 minute; add the remaining cream and then reduce until the mixture coats a spoon. Combine the endive mixture with the reduced sweetbreads/cream sauce and, if necessary, reduce to a creamy consistency. Adjust seasoning.

Place the sweetbreads on serving plates. Spoon endive sauce on top of the sweetbreads and garnish with additional whole endive leaves and fresh watercress.

SERVINGS: 4
PREPARATION TIME: 20 MINUTES (NOTE ELAPSED TIME)

MARINADE
1 boneless loin of venison,
   approximately 2 pounds
1 pint red wine
2 tablespoons olive oil
pinch of thyme
pinch of rosemary
pinch of garlic
1 bay leaf
pinch of juniper berries

Marinate the venison in the red wine, olive oil, herbs and juniper berries for 4 days in the refrigerator. Reserve one-half pint marinade.

SAUCE GRAND-VENEUR
4 pounds venison bones and
   trimmings
2 tablespoons olive oil
2 tablespoons clarified butter
1 carrot, diced
1 onion, diced
1 stalk celery, diced
1 pint red wine vinegar
2 pints Burgundy
3 quarts veal demi-glace (see page
   99)
crushed black pepper to taste

Brown the venison bones and trimmings in the oil and butter with the carrot, onion and celery. Season with crushed black pepper; add red wine vinegar and Burgundy. Reduce by three-fourths; add the demi-glace. Bring to a boil; then reduce heat and simmer for 3 hours. Strain sauce through a fine sieve and reserve, keeping warm.

CONFIT CHESTNUT
2 pounds fresh chestnuts
1 pound tinned duck fat

Make an incision in the shells and boil chestnuts in water for a few minutes. Remove from heat and peel off shell and skin. Slowly cook the chestnuts in the duck fat until tender. Reserve.

59

ASSEMBLY
2 ounces clarified butter
1 tablespoon red currant jelly
1 tablespoon fresh butter
salt and pepper to taste

Slice the venison loin into 8 medallions, each approximately 1-inch thick. Season both sides of the medallions with salt and pepper. Heat the clarified butter in a sauté pan to very hot. Place the medallions in the pan and cook 3 minutes on each side, to medium rare. Remove from pan; keep warm. Drain fat from the sauté pan and add the half pint reserved venison marinade. Reduce by three-fourths; add the prepared Sauce Grand-Veneur and reduce to desired thickness. Remove from heat and add the red currant jelly and fresh butter, agitating the pan as the butter melts. Strain the sauce and keep warm. Place confit chestnuts around the two medallions on each serving plate. Spoon sauce over the medallions and serve immediately.

RASPBERRY FEUILLETÉ

SERVINGS: 4
PREPARATION TIME: 25 MINUTES

CHANTILLY CREAM
 8 ounces heavy cream
 1 tablespoon powdered sugar
 ½ teaspoon vanilla
 1 teaspoon kirsch

Whip the cream until stiff. Fold in the sugar, vanilla and kirsch. Reserve in the refrigerator.

CARAMEL SAUCE
16 ounces sugar
 4 ounces water
 8 ounces heavy cream

Cook sugar and water until brown and syrupy. Stir in the cream and reserve, keeping warm.

ASSEMBLY
8 ounces puff pastry (purchase frozen and follow thawing instructions on package)
1 egg, beaten (egg wash)
1 pint fresh raspberries (strawberries may be substituted)

Roll out the puff pastry approximately ½-inch thick. Cut into four 4-inch squares. Brush with egg wash. Bake in a 425 degree oven for 20 minutes. Remove the pastry squares from the oven and split each in half horizontally. Pour a pool of caramel sauce on each serving plate. Place one pastry bottom on each plate and partially fill with chantilly cream. Top with raspberries. Garnish the plates with additional raspberries. Place tops of pastries next to bottoms and serve.

3 large eggs, separated
1 ounce Grand Marnier
zest (pith-free peel) of one orange,
  peeled
3⅓ ounces sugar
powdered sugar

Combine the egg yolks, Grand Marnier, orange zest and half the sugar in a mixing bowl. In another bowl, beat the egg whites to soft peaks; then add the remaining sugar and continue beating until stiff but not grainy. Fold the whites into the egg yolk mixture. Butter and sugar two soufflé molds, each approximately 4-inches in diameter. Fill the soufflé molds with the batter. Level off the tops and clean the rims. Bake in a 450 degree oven for 15 to 18 minutes. Sprinkle powdered sugar on top of the soufflés and serve immediately.

ROLAND LICCIONI
CARLOS' RESTAURANT

Within the spectrum of Oriental cooking, there are discernable French influences in the delicacy of Vietnamese food, a culinary reflection of the country's history. So when Vietnamese-born, French-raised Roland Liccioni approaches food at Carlos' Restaurant, in suburban Highland Park, there are nuances in the blending of flavors and presentation of his dishes relating to both cultures.

The restaurant is located in a white clapboard building which for fifty years housed a grocery store before its 1981 renovation to an intimate fifty-five-seat restaurant. The walls and banquettes are a soft, rich beige, accented by art deco touches such as etched glass and brass torchers mounted on the walls. The stylized decor extends to the table settings, where each service plate is a different pattern—part of the collection of owner Carlos Nieto's family.

The light, ecclectic look also is a reflection of Roland's food, primarily nouvelle French with influences from the Oriental market and memories of childhood in Southwest

France. His parents, who later in his life opened a Vietnamese restaurant, moved their family of fifteen children from Saigon to Biarritz in 1956. Although an avid soccer player, Roland decided at 13 to become a chef, and entered the École Hôtelière de Biarritz for a four-year training course.

"I loved sports but figured I would always have to eat. Working in a restaurant was a way to assure I would," he says.

At 17, he moved to Paris to work at the Bofinger Restaurant owned by Eric de Rothschild, and then returned briefly to Biarritz to climb the kitchen hierarchy at another restaurant, the Mandion Patissier.

His best training, working for the people he considers the developers of his style, was in the London kitchens of the Waterside Inn and La Gavroche, the famed restaurants of the Roux brothers.

"In France you have to work your station in the kitchen," he says, "and the Roux brothers not only taught me a lot about seasoning, pastry and sauces, but they gave me freedom to do things my own way that a French chef in France would never have done."

The Roux brothers wanted Roland, who was a sous chef, to remain with them when he received an offer from Alouette, a French restaurant in Chicago. "Something told me to see another country, and I took a chance, even though it was a difficult decision to make."

The cooking at Alouette, however, was a continuation of the style in which he was trained, and it was not until he had his own kitchen at Carlos' that Roland's personal philosophy began to emerge. He will use a jasmine tea sauce as a delicate topping to a soft-shelled crab appetizer, and is fond of using both ginger and lemon grass, two seasonings important in Vietnamese cooking. The sweet garlic sauce with which he tops duck, or the red pepper sauce used for a

combination of fresh grilled tuna and turbot, complemented by a three-mustard sauce, are his adaptations of those traditional French dishes.

The 28-year-old Roland, whose wife Mary Beth works with him in the kitchen, visits other restaurants in the United States whenever possible, although he inspires himself through his cooking, rather than gleaning ideas from others.

"When I was in school, I had to make a soufflé as part of my exam, and the teachers gave me 20 out of 20 on it," he says. "I was happy, but believe that nothing is ever perfect. I am trying always to make that 20 out of 20 with each plate that comes from my kitchen. But from each plate I am always learning, so I think the next one will be better." ✕

CARLOS'
HIGHLAND PARK

63

MENU

FLAN DE FOIE GRAS
A rich liver custard served with sherry wine vinegar sauce

RAVIOLI OF LANGOUSTINE
Ravioli with langoustine, spinach, shiitake mushroom filling, served with a langoustine sauce

ASSIETTE OF SQUAB WITH WILD MUSHROOMS
Roast breast and leg of squab with sautéed mixed vegetables and three types of wild mushrooms

NIGHT AND DAY CAKE
A chocolate cake with white chocolate mousse filling, topped with ganache

🏃

SERVINGS: 4
PREPARATION TIME: 1 HOUR

FLAN DE FOIE GRAS

FLAN
3½ ounces uncooked, domestic foie
    gras (if unavailable, cooked may
    be substituted)
1 ounce liver of duck, chicken or
    squab
⅛ teaspoon nutmeg, grated
½ small clove garlic, smashed
½ teaspoon flour
1 whole egg
1 egg yoke
2 tablespoons duck stock, reduced
    until syrupy (chicken stock may
    be substituted)
8 ounces milk
1 truffle, finely chopped
salt and pepper to taste

In a food processor, purée the foie gras and liver with the nutmeg, garlic and salt and pepper to taste. Add the flour. With the machine running, add the egg plus egg yolk. Add the reduced duck stock and the milk. The consistency should be very liquid. Strain the flan and correct the seasoning. Stir in the truffle. Pour the mixture into 4 or 5 buttered 2-ounce timbale molds. Set the molds in a pan which has been partially filled with hot water and bake in a 400 degree over for 25 minutes. Reserve keeping warm.

SAUCE

1 shallot, finely chopped
½ teaspoon truffle, chopped
3 teaspoons butter
1 tablespoon sherry wine vinegar
8 ounces duck stock, slightly
   reduced
1 teaspoon orange zest (pith-free
   peel), julienned
salt and pepper to taste

Sauté the shallot and truffle in 1 teaspoon butter. Deglaze the pan with the vinegar; then reduce until dry. Add the duck stock. Reduce to the desired consistency. Add the remaining butter, agitating the pan to melt and incorporate. Adjust the seasoning. Just before service, add the zest.

Unmold the flan. To serve, put one flan on each plate and top with sauce. If desired, add a slice of truffle and garnish with blanched asparagus tips.

SERVINGS: 4
PREPARATION TIME: 2 HOURS (NOTE ELAPSED TIME)

RAVIOLI OF LANGOUSTINE

PASTA AND FILLING

10 ounces flour
 3 eggs
few drops of olive oil
1 shallot, chopped
⅛ teaspoon ginger, chopped
1 tablespoon butter
5-6 medium shiitake mushrooms,
   stemmed and finely chopped
4-5 water chestnuts, finely chopped
8 large spinach leaves, blanched and
   refreshed
12 langoustines, peeled and deveined
   (discard stomach; reserve shell and
   any roe)
1 egg, beaten (egg wash)
salt and pepper to taste

Blend the flour and eggs in a food processor. Add the olive oil and mix until a ball of dough forms. On a floured board, briefly work the dough into a smooth ball. Cover with plastic wrap and refrigerate for 1½ hours.

Sauté the shallot and ginger in butter and then add the mushrooms and water chestnuts. Season with salt and pepper. Remove the mixture from heat and let cool. Using a pasta machine, roll out several thin sheets of pasta. Cut the pasta into 8 rectangles, approximately 3½-by-5-inches each, and place on a baking sheet lined with parchment paper. Place one spoonful of the mushroom mixture on each spinach leaf. Top each with a langoustine. Fold each leaf so that it covers the langoustine (leaves will not entirely encase the filling). Place one spinach-wrapped langoustine on each piece of pasta. Brush the egg wash on the pasta surrounding the spinach. Fold the pasta over the spinach and filling; pinch edges to seal. Trim with a pasta wheel. Refrigerate until use, up to one hour. Ravioli will hold in freezer for about 1 day.

Ravioli of Langoustine

SAUCE

1 tablespoon olive oil
reserved langoustine shell
1 tablespoon carrot, *chopped*
1 tablespoon shallot, *chopped*
1 tablespoon celery, *chopped*
1 tablespoon mushroom, *chopped*
1 tablespoon garlic, *chopped*
1 teaspoon tarragon
1 ounce cognac
2 ounces white wine
1 ounce sherry
¼ teaspoon black peppercorns,
    crushed
½ cup fish stock
1 cup cream
1 teaspoon tomato paste
reserved langoustine roe (optional)
1 tablespoon butter

To a very hot pan add the olive oil and then all of the langoustine shell.

Sauté about 1 minute; add carrot, shallot, celery, mushroom and garlic. After another mintue, add the tarragon. When shells are pink in color and vegetables are lightly browned, deglaze with cognac. Add the wine, sherry and crushed peppercorns. Reduce until almost dry. Add fish stock. Briefly reduce again and then add cream and tomato paste. Simmer gently for 10 to 15 minutes to thicken. Strain the sauce. Just before service, add the roe; then add butter, agitating the pan to melt and incorporate.

ASSEMBLY

Cook the ravioli in salted boiling water for 7 minutes. Remove the ravioli from the water with a slotted spoon and drain. Place 2 ravioli per

(continued)

66

person on serving plates. Spoon the sauce over the ravioli and garnish each plate with a langoustine (cooked in salted water for approximately 4 minutes). Sprinkle chopped chives over the ravioli and serve.

SERVINGS: 4
PREPARATION TIME: 45 MINUTES

SQUAB AND SAUCE
4 whole squabs, 1 pound each
2 tablespoons clarified butter
1 tablespoon fresh butter
1 tablespoon mushrooms, chopped
1 tablespoon shallots, chopped
1 tablespoon garlic, chopped
1 tablespoon celery, chopped
1 tablespoon carrot, chopped
1 teaspoon thyme
1 ounce cognac
2 ounces white wine
2 cups duck stock (any other stock may be substituted)
2 teaspoons fresh butter
salt and pepper to taste

Remove and debone the breast and legs from the squab. Season with salt and pepper. Chop the remaining carcass and reserve. Heat to very hot 1 tablespoon clarified butter in an ovenproof sauté pan. Add the breasts and legs, placing them skinside down. Add fresh butter and quickly brown both sides (do not overcook). Place the pan in a 450 degree oven for 3 to 4 minutes. When medium rare, remove from oven and reserve, keeping warm.

Place 1 tablespoon clarified butter and reserved chopped carcass in a heated saucepan. When bones are thoroughly browned, add mushroom, shallot, garlic, celery and carrot. Sauté the vegetables until lightly browned; add thyme. When a glaze forms on the bottom of the pan, deglaze with cognac. Add white wine and reduce for 2 to 3 minutes. Add the duck stock; gently simmer for 20 minutes. Strain the sauce; bring back to a boil and reduce until thick enough to coat a spoon, skimming occasionally. Then add 2 teaspoons fresh butter. Reserve, keeping warm.

MIXED VEGETABLE GARNISH
1 tablespoon olive oil
½ small eggplant, peeled and finely diced
½ clove garlic, minced
1 small red pepper, finely diced
1 small zucchini, finely diced
1 shallot, minced
pinch of rosemary
salt to taste

Heat the olive oil in a sauté pan. Add vegetables and briefly cook with the seasonings to al dente.

MUSHROOM GARNISH
3 shiitake mushrooms, stemmed and halved
3 hedgehog mushrooms, halved
3 pleurotte mushrooms, halved
1 tablespoon clarified butter
salt to taste

Sauté mushrooms in clarified butter until tender. Season with salt to taste. Reserve, keeping warm.

Divide the mixed vegetable garnish and the mushroom garnish among four heated serving plates. Slice the squab breasts and arrange pinwheel fashion on each plate around the legs. Ladle the sauce on the squab and serve.

CHOCOLATE CAKE

⅔ ounce cornstarch
⅔ ounce cake flour
⅔ ounce cocoa
5 eggs, separated
few drops of lemon juice
4 ounces sugar

Sift together cornstarch, cake flour and cocoa. Set aside. Beat the egg whites and lemon juice at high speed to soft peaks. Add sugar and continue to beat until stiff peaks form. Slightly beat egg yolks and manually fold into whites. Gradually fold in dry ingredients, being careful not to deflate egg whites. Pour the batter into a buttered and floured 10-inch round pan. Bake in a 350 degree oven for 30 minutes or until the sides of the cake pull away slightly from the pan.

GANACHE

8 ounces semi-sweet chocolate
2 tablespoons soft butter

Melt the chocolate in the top of a double boiler over warm water. Whisk in the butter. Reserve.

SYRUP

2 ounces sugar
2 ounces water
1 ounce dark rum or Grand Marnier

Bring the sugar and water to a boil. Remove from heat and cool. Add the liquor. The syrup will keep indefinitely in a covered jar in the refrigerator.

WHITE CHOCOLATE MOUSSE

2½ ounces sugar
¼ cup water
2 egg yolks
1 whole egg
1 teaspoon sugar
2 tablespoons dark rum
1 tablespoon Grand Marnier
1 envelope (¼ ounce) unflavored gelatin, dissolved in ¼ cup cold water
2½ ounces white chocolate, melted in a double boiler over warm water
10 ounces whipping cream

In a small pan combine 2½ ounces sugar and ¼ cup water and cook to 248 degrees (hard-ball stage). In a round-bottomed mixing bowl, combine the egg yolks, whole egg, 1 teaspoon sugar, 1 tablespoon dark rum and 1 tablespoon Grand Marnier. On the stove, set the mixing bowl over a pan of warm water (160 to 170 degrees) and constantly beat the mixture until it is warm and foamy. Add the dissolved gelatin; whisk to incorporate. Remove from heat and, using a mixer set at slow speed, gradually add the sugar and water (cooked to the hard-ball stage). Continue to mix at slow speed until the mixture is completely cool. Then add the melted white chocolate. In another bowl, whip the cream to stiff peaks; add some to the chocolate mixture; fold in the remainder. Add 1 tablespoon dark rum for flavor. To avoid loss of volume, use as soon as possible.

ASSEMBLY

*2 tablespoons white raisins, halved
and soaked in dark rum*

Slice the cake into 2 layers. Spread half the ganache on one of the layers. Invert the layer into a 10-inch round pan (so the ganache is on the bottom) lined with plastic wrap. Brush the layer of cake with half of the syrup. Then sprinkle with rum-soaked raisins and top with the white chocolate mousse. Place the other layer of cake in the mold and brush it with the remaining syrup. Spread ganache on top and refrigerate 6 hours to overnight. Invert and unmold the cake onto a serving plate. Decorate as desired and serve.

THIÉRRY LEFEUVRE
FROGGY'S

American diners frequently equate French cooking with crystal chandeliers and exorbitant dinner checks. But at Froggy's in suburban Highwood, Thiérry Lefeuvre has been proving for four years that there is more to French cooking than truffles and *foie gras*, and offers a six-course dinner for less than $20—the cost of the entrée alone in other French restaurants.

"French people don't eat in expensive three-star restaurants every day, but even if they're going to a neighborhood bistro they want good food," he says.

Because of the moderate pricing, many o the customers at Froggy's are regulars. Thiérry changes the menu monthly. He doesn't want his customers to tire of any dishes, and his own sense of experimentation makes him want to keep inventing.

Thiérry's background, from the farming country of Brittany where he was born thirty-three years ago, is where his sense o taste first developed. His mother was an ar ist, and Sunday dinner was the family's cu nary highlight. "Something different each week that would fascinate your palate," he remembers.

He entered the École Hôtelière in Tours, studying cooking for three years and serving for an additonal year. While Thiérry has never studied with any of the stars of the French culinary constellation, he credits the chefs at the Grand Hôtel du Parc in Switzerland and those commanding the kitchens of restaurants in St. Tropez with giving him an appreciation for the techniques of cooking and the management of a kitchen.

Not only did he move from restaurant to restaurant, he also worked for two years as chef to the governor of Tahiti, before going back to school—this time in Montreal—to add business acumen to his culinary prowess. Before moving to Chicago to become chef at Alouette, owned by the same owners as Froggy's, he was chef for two years at Hôtel La Sapinière in Canada.

"When I started at Alouette I was only 25 years old, and although I was trained there was so much more to learn," he says. "So I started reading a lot of books and food magazines from around the world to learn about the development of nouvelle cuisine, so much of which is part of my style now."

Froggy's carries its whimsical name through to the shape of the salt and pepper shakers on the tables covered with green oilcloth. Frogs also are depicted around the bar, although the small floral tapestry on the banquettes makes the room more formal. Froggy's huge kitchen is much larger than most restaurants with its seating capacity, but it takes into account the volume of food prepared. Froggy's, which takes no reservations, generally will seat tables three times on a weekend night.

"I will never sacrifice quality," Thiérry says, "but I am very careful when I am doing the buying, and always in search of new dishes with a reasonable food cost. I know there are chefs who never consider cost, and sometimes I envy them, but I think of costs as part of the challenge of cooking."

And diners are never aware of the careful balancing act. For dishes requiring expensive ingredients, such as a trademark dish of lobster in a delicate sauce flavored with vanilla, there are dishes made with less tender but succulent cuts of meat, such as skirt steak or slowly simmered tripe.

"I will never put ingredients together because I like the look of a dish," says Thiérry, who turns from businessman to artist once in the kitchen. "The look, yes, is very important to me, but if I was interested in colors alone I would just do paintings. I am a chef, so the dishes have to follow through with flavors that will excite the palate, too." ✗

FROGGY'S
HIGHWOOD

MENU

SEAFOOD AND HERB SAUSAGE
Sausages of shrimp, salmon, and bay scallops served with seed mustard sauce

LOBSTER IN VANILLA SAUCE
Boiled Maine lobster garnished with leeks, served with vanilla sauce

BELGIAN ENDIVE SALAD WITH SWEET ONION CONFIT
Salad of Belgian endives with a warm red onion garnish, served with raspberry vinegar dressing

BREAST OF DUCK WITH GREEN PEPPERCORN SAUCE
Sliced, sautéed breast of duck garnished with wild mushrooms, served with green peppercorn sauce

LEMON MOUSSE IN A PASTRY SHELL
A tangy mousse garnished with kiwi, served with black currant sauce

✗

SERVINGS: 4 (about 8 5-inch sausages)
PREPARATION TIME: 40 MINUTES

SEAFOOD AND HERB SAUSAGE

SAUSAGE
- 1 pound salmon fillet, chopped
- 1 pound sea scallops (with or without roe)
- 2 egg whites
- 2 pinches of chives
- 2 pinches of basil
- 2 pinches of tarragon
- ½ quart whipping cream
- ½ pound small shrimp, peeled and deveined (both cooked and uncooked will work)
- sausage casings
- 3 quarts fish stock
- salt and pepper to taste

In a food processor, purée the salmon, half of the sea scallops, egg whites, herbs, salt and pepper. With the machine running, add the cream. Put the mixture into a bowl. Rough chop the remaining sea scallops. Add chopped scallops, scallop roe (if available) and shrimp, to the purée. Season with salt and pepper. Pipe the mixture into sausage casings, making sure the casings are tightly packed. Twist the ends and tie with string. Simmer 5 to 10 minutes in heated fish stock (almost to cover), turning occasionally. Cool to room temperature.

SEED MUSTARD SAUCE
pinch of basil
pinch of tarragon
pinch of chives
1 teaspoon Dijon mustard
1 egg yolk
1 teaspoon seed mustard
1 ounce red wine vinegar
2 ounces salad oil
salt and pepper to taste

In a bowl, combine the herbs, Dijon mustard and egg yolk. Whisk in the seed mustard and red wine vinegar. While whisking, add the salad oil. Season to taste with salt and pepper.

Remove the sausages from the casings and slice. Serve on individual serving plates. Spoon seed mustard sauce around the sausage and garnish with chives, basil, and, if desired, 1 large boiled shrimp.

SERVINGS: 4
PREPARATION TIME: 2 HOURS

COURT BOUILLON AND LOBSTER
1 carrot, roughly chopped
1 large onion, roughly chopped
1 stalk celery, roughly chopped
few parsley stems
1 clove garlic
4-5 black peppercorns
2 bay leaves
pinch of thyme
pinch of tarragon
salt to taste
½ gallon fish stock or water
1 vanilla bean, sliced in half
   lengthwise
½ gallon white wine
2-3 branches seaweed
2 lobsters, about 1½ pounds each

Simmer all the ingredients through the fish stock or water for 1 hour. Add the vanilla bean and white wine and bring to a boil. Add the seaweed and lobsters and boil 8 to 10 minutes. Reserve until service.

VANILLA SAUCE
3-4 shallots, chopped
½ teaspoon butter
2 ounces white wine
1 vanilla bean, chopped
1 quart whipping cream
1 ounce fish glacé (1 ounce of lobster
   tomalley may be substituted)
1 pound bay scallops
salt and pepper to taste

Briefly sauté shallots in butter. Add white wine and vanilla bean. Reduce until almost dry. Add cream and fish glacé. Bring to a boil. Reduce heat and simmer about 5 minutes. At the last minute, add the scallops just to warm. Correct seasoning. Remove pan from heat and reserve, keeping warm.

LOBSTER IN VANILLA
SAUCE

Lobster in Vanilla Sauce

LEEK GARNISH
*1 leek, chopped (use all of the white
   part and 2 inches of the green)*
1 tablespoon butter
6 ounces whipping cream
salt and pepper to taste

Sauté the leek in the butter until
tender but still green in color. Add
the whipping cream. Season with
salt and pepper and reduce at a low
boil until the liquid almost evaporates
and a thick sauce forms. Reserve,
keeping warm.

Shell the lobster tails and claws.
Slice the tails into medallions. On
each serving plate place 1 spoonful of
leeks and half of a lobster. Spoon
scallops on top of the leeks. Spoon
vanilla sauce over all. Garnish with
lobster heads, tails, and legs.

ONION CONFIT
1 ounce oil
1 sweet red onion, sliced
3 raspberries (fresh or frozen)
1 ounce raspberry vinegar
salt and pepper to taste

In a sauté pan, heat the oil until hot.
Add onion and sauté about 1 minute.
Season with salt and pepper. Add
the raspberries and the raspberry
vinegar. Briefly cook until onions
are tender yet still crisp.

DRESSING
pinch of chives
pinch of tarragon
1 ounce raspberry vinegar
1 teaspoon Dijon mustard
1 egg yolk
1 raspberry
2 ounces salad oil
salt and pepper

Whisk together all the ingredients
through the egg yolk. While whisking, add the raspberry and oil. Correct the seasoning.

ASSEMBLY
2 firm Belgian endives
½ teaspoon parsley, chopped
1 head oak leaf lettuce

Trim the base of the endives. Wash
and separate the leaves. Toss with
the parsley in the prepared dressing.
Add the onion confit. Arrange on a
bed of oak leaf lettuce and serve.

BREAST OF DUCK WITH GREEN PEPPERCORN SAUCE

SERVINGS: 4
PREPARATION TIME: 2 HOURS

DUCK AND SAUCE

   2 ducks, 5-6 pounds each
   5 ounces rendered duck fat
   2 carrots, chopped
   2 stalks celery, chopped
   1 clove garlic
3-4 sprigs parsley
   2 Spanish onions, chopped
   1 teaspoon coarsely ground black
      pepper
   2 bay leaves
   1 teaspoon thyme
1½ teaspoons green peppercorns
   ½ liter red wine
   1 gallon duck or veal stock
   8 baby carrots with tops, peeled
salt and pepper to taste

Remove duck breasts and trim skin and fat. Remove legs and save for another dish of your choice. Chop and reserve the carcass and wings. Reserve and render the fat.

Put 3 ounces of the rendered duck fat into a large saucepan. Add the carrots, celery, garlic, parsley and onions and sauté until lightly browned. Add the reserved duck bones, black pepper, bay leaves, thyme and 1 teaspoon of the green peppercorns. Cook until the bones are well browned. Add the red wine and all but 4 ounces of the duck or veal stock. Bring to a boil and simmer 1 hour. Strain the sauce. Add the remaining ½ teaspoon green peppercorns and simmer 5 to 10 minutes to preferred thickness.

In a sauté pan, heat the remaining 2 ounces of rendered duck fat. Season the duck breasts with salt and pepper and place in the hot pan. Sauté, turning occasionally. Add the baby carrots. When the duck is medium rare, remove from the pan and reserve in a warm place. With the carrots still in the pan, drain off excess grease. Add 4 ounces of veal or duck stock and simmer for a few minutes to form a glaze. Remove from heat and reserve.

MUSHROOM GARNISH

   4 teaspoons butter
   2 shallots, chopped
15 ounces mixed wild mushrooms,
      cleaned and sliced (a combination
      of shiitake, oyster, and mutton foot
      works well)
   1 teaspoon parsley, chopped
salt and pepper to taste

Briefly sauté shallots in 2 teaspoons melted butter. Add the sliced mushrooms. Season with salt and pepper. Midway through cooking, add the remaining 2 teaspoons of butter. When the mushrooms are almost done, add the parsley. Remove from heat and reserve.

Slice the breasts and arrange on serving plates. Garnish with baby carrots and mushrooms. Spoon sauce on the plate and serve.

LEMON MOUSSE
6 ounces lemon juice
zest (pith-free peel) of two lemons,
    chopped
7 ounces sugar
2½ ounces water
1 envelope (¼ ounce) unflavored
    gelatin
16 ounces whipping cream

Combine the lemon juice, zest, sugar and water in a saucepan. Bring mixture to a boil; then sprinkle with gelatin, and stir. Bring mixture back to a boil and remove from heat. Completely cool over a bowl of ice, stirring constantly. Beat the whipping cream until stiff. Strain the cooled lemon mixture into whipped cream. Fold together; whisk briskly. Reserve.

PASTRY SHELL
2 ounces almonds
2 ounces flour
3½ ounces soft butter
3½ ounces powdered sugar
3 egg whites
1 ounce vanilla extract

Toast 2 ounces of almonds by spreading them on a baking sheet and baking in a 350 degree oven for 5 to 10 minutes, watching them carefully to prevent burning. Cool at room temperature; blend in a food processor with ⅓ ounce of the flour (of the total 2 ounces called for) until a powder forms.

With a mixer on slow speed, combine the butter, powdered sugar, almond powder and egg whites. Beat at medium speed for 2 minutes. While beating, slowly add the re-maining flour. Scrape down the sides; then add the vanilla and beat at medium speed another 30 seconds until the batter is smooth. Generously butter a baking sheet. Put batter into a pastry bag; pipe twelve 5- to 6-inch circles (depending on the size of the mold you plan to use) onto the prepared baking sheet, allowing plenty of space between circles. Spread the batter slightly with a knife. Bake in a preheated 375 degree oven for 3 to 4 minutes, checking frequently, until pastry is golden brown yet pliable. Remove from the oven and immediately mold the pastry in deep saucers or shallow bowls, shaping the sides. Let rest until the pastry hardens.

BLACK CURRANT COULIS
6 ounces black currants
2 ounces sugar
6 ounces water
2 ounces cassis liqueur

Combine the ingredients in a saucepan. Bring to a boil. Cool, strain and reserve.

ASSEMBLY
4 kiwis, peeled and sliced
2 ounces lemon marmalade, melted

Pour the lemon mousse into the pastry shells. Carfully slide each pastry shell out of its mold and onto a serving plate. Spoon black currant coulis around the filled shell. Place slices of kiwi on top of the lemon mousse and around the shell on the plate. Brush lemon marmalade on top of the kiwi in the pastry shell and serve.

LUCIEN VERGE
L'ESCARGOT

While many French restaurants have been transformed by the influence of nouvelle cuisine, Lucien Verge's L'Escargot has remained a bastion for the simple, honest food of provincial French cooking.

In fact, customers are so thrilled by his cassoulet that they do not allow him to remove it from the menu, even during the warm summer months. And his desserts, rather than being elaborate constructions, feature the elegant simplicity of fruit—fruit tarts and feathery crêpes filled with fresh fruit.

"I call my style of cooking *cuisine du terroir*," says the 52-year-old native of Lyons. "It means cooking of the earth; and, when it appears on the plate it is basic, country cooking."

But traditional and authentic dishes also can be done with the finest and freshest ingredients, and this is equally important to Lucien. When he first moved to Chicago in 1966, he was unable to find French mustard in the markets and had to send to New York for many ingredients. Those he could not locate he would work around, and devise new dishes in his traditional idiom rather than settle for less than the best.

Lucien maintains he has not changed, but his customers have finally caught up with him. "A few years ago I couldn't get them to try dishes like *choucroute* with braised cabbage and sausages, or a *pot au feu* with boiled meats, but they trust me, and if I go into the dining room and suggest a dish, they're likely to give it a chance."

While his style of cooking cycles back to his childhood, his training was in the grand tradition. After four years at La Mere Filloux in his native Lyons, starting training when he was 16, Lucien moved to the dining rooms of two of Paris' finest hotels, the Hotel Crillion and the Hôtel Plaza Athenée.

"A chef's trade is not all written in a book, and each place I worked opened up a different part of the repertoire of French cooking," he says.

The varying size of the restaurants also added to his training. While his experience in Lyons—one of the gastronomic centers of France—was small, and he had a variety of duties, the kitchen at the Plaza Athenée had 43 chefs, so he assimilated the structure needed to avoid chaos while feeding a large number of people.

From Paris he moved to New York in 1956 to work at Le Veau d'Or, a restaurant known for the same informal and hearty style of cooking Lucien produces today. Dishes such as leg of lamb and roast duckling were favorites, and he became aware of Americans' taste.

"It was during those years that I really came to understand recipes from my heart and not just my head," he says. "You cannot just follow a recipe, you have to understand what each ingredient does to it."

This innate feeling for cooking was immediately appreciated when L'Escargot opened on Halsted Street in 1968. The eighty-five-

seat restaurant, in subtle tones of blues and grays, was destroyed by fire in 1979. Lucien and his partner, Alan Tutzer, opened a second location, one seating more than 200 diners, off the lobby of the Allerton Hotel in the heart of the city's business district in 1980. Three years later, the original reopened, and Lucien now splits his time between the two.

Both restaurants are related not only in terms of the menu, but in the gifts from customers which decorate them—snails in every artistic medium from watercolor to woven rattan.

Lucien's penchant for preserving the authenticity of French food separates him from many of his contemporaries, whose styles are praised for their sense of adventure. He prides himself on his ability to communicate the foods from which other chefs are basing their innovations.

"I say to myself, 'I do it authentically,' and then I try to convince people that this is the way they should eat." ✗

L'ESCARGOT
CHICAGO

MENU

SNAIL TOURTE COUNTRY STYLE
A pie filled with sautéed snails, leeks and ham in a salted custard

MEDALLIONS OF VENISON WITH TRUFFLED POTATOES
*Marinated tenderloin of venison napped in a rich red wine sauce,
served with truffled Potatoes Dauphine*

DESSERT IN ALL SIMPLICITY
*A pair of tartelettes—one filled with fresh berries and another
with chestnut filling and ganache*

PEAR CRÊPES
Poached pears in French crêpes topped with toasted almonds and flamed with pear brandy

𐀴

SERVINGS: 6 AS APPETIZER, 4 AS ENTREE
PREPARATION TIME: 1½ HOURS

SNAIL TOURTE COUNTRY STYLE

PIE AND FILLING
  1 cup leeks (about 4), white part
    only, julienned
  4 ounces butter
  1 cup water
  ½ cup white wine
  6 ounces boiled ham, julienned
  2 cloves garlic, minced
  2 teaspoons parsley, chopped
  2 ounces shallots, chopped
  2 dozen canned snails (72 count),
    drained and rinsed
coarsely ground black pepper to taste
  2 pounds puff pastry (purchase
    frozen and thaw according to
    instructions on package)
  1 egg, beaten with 1 tablespoon
    water, cream or milk (egg wash)
  3 whole eggs
  2 egg yolks

pinch of nutmeg
1½ cups half and half
salt and white pepper to taste

Sauté the leeks slowly in 1 ounce butter for about 5 minutes, until tender but not browned. Add water and wine and boil about 20 minutes, until completely reduced and leeks are tender. (Depending on the season, it may be necessary to add more water to the leeks to cook them to tender.) Briefly sauté the ham in 1 ounce butter to release flavor. Remove from heat and reserve.

Combine the remaining 2 ounces butter with the garlic, parsley and shallots to form garlic butter. Sauté the snails in the garlic butter for 2 to

(continued)

80

Snail Tourte Country Style

3 minutes. Remove from heat and season the snails with coarsely-ground black pepper. Completely cool the leeks, ham and snails.

Roll out the puff pastry to ¼-inch thick. Cut out 2 circles, each about 13 inches in diameter. Place one circle of pastry into an 11-inch tart pan (preferably one with a removable rim) and shape to fit the pan. Prick the pastry with a fork. Place the cooled leeks, ham and snails on the pastry. Cover with the other circle of pastry. Moisten the edges of the dough with water; then press the two sheets together. Pinch edges to seal. Brush the top of pie with egg wash. Cut a 1-inch hole in the center of the top crust and place an aluminum foil tube in it to keep the hole open during baking.

Bake in a 375 degree oven for 15 minutes. Beat the whole eggs plus egg yolks with the nutmeg and salt and pepper. Whisk in the half and half. After 15 minutes, remove the pie from the oven and pour the egg mixture quickly but carefully into the pie through the aluminum foil tube (tilt and rotate the tart pan, making sure the pie is filled but not overflowing with the mixture. Lower the oven temperature to 350 degrees. Return the pie to the oven and bake for 30 to 40 minutes until the center is set and the pastry is browned. Let the pie rest about 15 to 20 minutes in a warm place before serving.

BUERRE NANTAIS SAUCE
  2 shallots, chopped
  ½ cup white wine
  ¼ cup white wine vinegar
  ½ cup whipping cream
  8 ounces sweet butter
  1½ teaspoons parsley, chopped
  1 teaspoon chives, chopped
salt and white pepper to taste

In a saucepan, combine the shallots, wine and vinegar. Reduce until dry, about 10 to 15 minutes. Add the cream; whisk in the butter bit by bit. Season with salt and white pepper. Strain the sauce into a warm tureen; then stir in the parlsey and chives.

Serve slices of snail tourte with Beurre Nantais Sauce on the side.

MEDALLIONS OF VENISON WITH TRUFFLED POTATOES

SERVINGS: 6-8
PREPARATION TIME: 5 HOURS (NOTE ELAPSED TIME)

MEDALLIONS OF VENISON
  2 tenderloins of venison,
    approximately 1 pound each
  1 bottle full-bodied red wine
  1 stalk celery, roughly chopped
  1 leek, roughly chopped
  1 onion, roughly chopped
  1 carrot, roughly chopped
  1 clove garlic
  2 bay leaves
sprig of parsley
pinch of thyme
3-4 juniper berries (if available)
  1 ounce red wine vinegar
  3 tablespoons oil
  3 ounces butter
½ teaspoon shallots, chopped
dash of cognac
  2 ounces veal demi-glace
    (see page 99)
  1 teaspoon red currant jelly (or to
    taste)
¼ cup whipping cream
salt and coarsely ground black pepper
    to taste

Marinate the tenderloins in the ingredients through red wine vinegar, plus 1 tablespoon of oil for 24 hours in the refrigerator. Remove the tenderloins from the marinade and, cutting slightly on the bias, slice 8 medallions, each approximately 1-inch thick. Strain and reserve 1½ cups marinade. Pat the medallions dry with paper towel. Season both sides with salt and pepper; sauté in 2 tablespoons oil and 1 ounce butter until cooked to preference.

Remove meat from pan and keep warm and covered. Drain the fat from the sauté pan. Add 2 ounces butter and the shallots. Deglaze with cognac and add the reserved 1½ cups of marinade. Reduce about 10 minutes, to one-half the volume. Add the demi-glace. Taste and sweeten with red currant jelly. Add the cream and reduce to desired consistency. Adjust the seasoning with salt and pepper. Place 2 medallions on each plate and strain the sauce over them. Serve with truffled potatoes (see recipe below). Other garnishes might include fresh artichoke bottoms sautéed in butter and filled with diced, sautéed wild mushrooms; and braised Boston lettuce.

TRUFFLED POTATOES

1 pound Idaho potatoes
1 cup pâte à choux (cream puff
  pastry), (see recipe below)
2 whole truffles, diced (2 ounces
  grated Swiss cheese can be
  substituted)

Peel potatoes. Boil in salted water
until tender; then mash (you should
have 2 cups of mashed potatoes).
Dry the potatoes for 5 minutes in a
350 degree oven to remove moisture.
Remove from the oven; add pâte à
choux and mix together. Stir in truffles. Drop by spoonfuls into a deep-
fat fryer preheated to 425 degrees.
Fry for 3 to 4 minutes, until golden
brown. Serve immediately.

PÂTE À CHOUX

1 cup milk
3 ounces butter
pinch of salt
1 cup flour
4-5 eggs, depending on the size

Bring the milk, butter and salt to
boil. Add the flour all at once and
mix vigorously with a wooden spoon
until the paste becomes dry and pulls
away from the side of the pan. Remove from heat and add the eggs,
one or two at a time, mixing until
incorporated and smooth.

SERVINGS: 4
PREPARATION TIME: 40 MINUTES (NOTE ELAPSED TIME)

PASTRY

  4 ounces flour
  1 ounce sugar
2½ ounces soft butter
  2 egg yolks
dash of salt

On a pastry board or table, make a
well in the flour. Place the sugar and
butter in the well and incorporate
into the flour. Add the egg yolks and
salt and work the dough until the
ingredients are well blended and
a smooth ball is formed. Cover the
dough and let rest in the refrigerator
for a few hours or overnight.

On a floured board, roll out the
dough, adding as little flour as possible in the process, until it is the thickness of a silver dollar. Fill eight oval
tartelette molds, 4- to 5-inches each,
with the pastry. Prick the bottoms of
the pastry with a fork and fill each
mold with any type of dried beans
(to keep the shape of the mold while
baking). Bake in a 350 degree oven
for approximately 15 minutes (remove
molds from the oven when the crust
is slightly golden but is still soft in
the center; the pastry will finish baking outside the oven). Let the shells
cool slightly. Remove the dried
beans. Unmold the pastry and
reserve.

FRUIT GLAZE

½ cup raspberries
½ cup powdered sugar

Purée the berries with the sugar. Strain and reserve.

CHESTNUT FILLING

2 tablespoons chestnut purée
2 tablespoons chestnut spread
2 tablespoons soft butter
2 tablespoons dark rum or kirsch
dash of almond extract

Mix chestnut purée and chestnut spread with the butter. Add the rum and the almond extract. Reserve.

CHOCOLATE GANACHE

6 ounces semi-sweet chocolate
1 ounce sweet butter
¾ cup whipping cream

In the top of a double boiler, melt the chocolate. Add the butter. Remove from heat and whisk in the whipping cream. Reserve.

ASSEMBLY

½ cup fresh raspberries (stemmed and halved fresh strawberries may be substituted)
powdered sugar

Fill 4 of the pastry tartelettes with a mound of chestnut filling and place in the freezer for 15 to 20 minutes. Remove from the freezer and cover the tops with chocolate ganache. Refrigerate for 15 minutes before serving. Brush the inside of the 4 remaining tartelettes with the fruit glaze. Arrange the fresh berries inside the pastry and dust with powdered sugar just before serving. Serve each person one fruit and one chestnut tartelette.

POACHED PEARS

4 pears, peeled, cored and halved
(with stems left on)
1 cup sugar
dash of vanilla
juice of ½ lemon
water to cover

Combine the ingredients in a sauce-pan. Poach the pears until tender. Cool to room temperature and reserve.

CRÊPES

4 ounces flour
2 ounces sugar
3 eggs, slightly beaten
2 tablespoons oil
2½ ounces butter, melted and lightly
browned (plus a scant amount for
cooking crêpes)
1½ cups milk
dash of salt
dash of orange blossom water

Mix together the flour, sugar, eggs and oil. Stir in the melted butter, milk, salt and orange blossom water. Let the batter rest 15 minutes. Heat a skillet or crêpe pan; brush pan lightly with butter and pour in enough batter to cover the bottom with a thin coating. Cook crêpes about 1 minute each, until brown. Turn and brown the other side, about 30 seconds. Repeat, making eight crêpes in all. Reserve in a warm place.

ASSEMBLY

2 ounces apricot preserves, melted,
strained and cooled
1 ounce slivered almonds, toasted
powdered sugar
2 ounces pear brandy or Cointreau

Brush apricot glaze on each crêpe. Place a pear half, cored side down, on one half of each crêpe. Fold the other side of the crêpe over the pear. Place two pear-filled crêpes on each ovenproof serving plate. Brush the edge of the crêpes with some of the poaching liquid. Sprinkle crêpes with almonds and sugar; place in a 375 degree oven for 5 minutes. Before serving, pour some pear brandy over each crêpe and flame.

YOSHI KATSUMURA
YOSHI'S CAFÉ

At the same time Western chefs began embracing the simple elegance of Japanese food, the Japanese were developing an appetite for the rich and complex nature of classic French cooking. It was in the French restaurants of Tokyo that Yoshi Katsumura learned the dicta of Escoffier, a foundation that served him well when he immigrated to Chicago in 1972 and began commanding a series of fine French kitchens.

"I was so impressed by the taste of French food," he says. "Japanese food is very simple, and the first time I tried dishes like boeuf bourguignon I became so intrigued."

But strictly French cooking did not allow for the emergence of his Japanese spirit, so the food at Yoshi's Café, the forty-seat restaurant he opened in November 1982, could be best termed Franco-Japanese. The Oriental influences can be as subtle as the angle at which a roll of rare grilled tuna is sliced, so that it resembles sashimi, or the choice of Japanese porcelain bowls in which he arranges sole, scallop mousse and medallions of lobster.

"I keep the Oriental influence second in my food, but sometimes other people notice things I take for granted," he says. "Customers who are used to someone with a French eye arranging the plates tell me they notice the difference."

The interior of the restaurant—where his wife, Nobuko, runs the dining room—is as subtle as Yoshi's food. The floor is covered with old-fashioned hexagonal tiles; the walls are painted soft beige. A gleaming brass rail separates a raised seating area along one wall, papered in the same random floral print as the entry. In the foyer is the plaque recognizing the restaurant as a Mobil Travel Guide Four-Star winner, and certificates lauding Yoshi's as a *Chicago* magazine Top Ten restaurant.

Both the setting and food are lighter than those of Yoshi's past. Born and raised in Ibaraki, Japan, just a few hours north of Tokyo, he always liked cooking, although his only professional experience was working in a Chinese restaurant kitchen.

At age 19, the now-35-year-old chef began a series of apprenticeships in the French restaurants of Tokyo gaining popularity at that time. "I learned the basics of classic cooking in a very classic system," he says. "I started as a dishwasher and then went to peeling vegetables."

His dream was to work in France, but, when no jobs materialized he took advantage of an opportunity to move to Chicago. Once there in 1972, he started working at Le Bastille. In three years, he had worked his way through the ranks to chef, and then moved to La Reserve for a year.

Like many chefs in Chicago, Yoshi worked under the tutelage of Jean Banchet at Le Français for a year, in 1977. But he had yet to experience French food on French soil, and so decided to work for a year in Paris and Lyons.

When Yoshi returned to Chicago he became chef and a partner at Jimmy's Place, then considered one of the city's finest and most innovative French restaurants. "At Jimmy's I had freedom, and that was where I developed the style of cooking now served at Yoshi's. A contrast of textures, like those found in Japanese food, became very important to me. I like to put together dishes with little bits of the best of all cultures."

After changing cultures himself, Yoshi is a keen observer of how American culture is changing. "Food is fashion, and for a chef to remain popular with the public he has to catch the fashion as it is changing and try to stay ahead of it," he says. "Now it is food that is light, but I think in five years what I would like to do is run a restaurant like a French brasserie." ✕

YOSHI'S CAFÉ
CHICAGO

MENU

HOT DUCK PÂTÉ IN PUFF PASTRY

Pâté of marinated duck, pork and veal, baked in a puff pastry, served with Sauce Perigueux

DOVER SOLE WITH SCALLOP MOUSSE AND MEDALLIONS OF LOBSTER

Foil packages of Dover sole fillet and scallop mousse, simmered in court bouillon, served with herb butter sauce

ROAST BREAST OF PHEASANT STUFFED WITH PHEASANT MOUSSE AND FOIE GRAS

A rich mousse accented with truffles in a pheasant breast pocket, served with shiitake mushroom sauce

GREEN TEA ICE CREAM

Homemade ice cream delicately flavored with powdered Japanese green tea, served with fresh raspberry sauce

✘

1 duck, approximately 4 pounds
½ pound pork butt, cubed
½ pound veal shoulder, cubed
pinch of nutmeg
pinch of allspice
pinch of thyme
1 bay leaf
8 ounces white wine
2 cloves garlic, unpeeled
2 eggs
1 ounce truffles, chopped
¼ pound pistachio nuts, blanched,
   skins removed
¼ cup duck glaze
1 tablespoon truffle juice
12 ounces foie gras
1 truffle, thinly sliced (optional)
2 pounds puff pastry (purchase
   frozen and thaw according to
   instructions on package)
1 egg, beaten with 1 tablespoon milk
   or cream (egg wash)
salt and pepper to taste

Remove meat from legs and breast of duck. Remove all skin and fat. Marinate duck meat, pork butt and veal shoulder with nutmeg, allspice, thyme, bay leaf, wine and garlic for 3 or 4 days in the refrigerator. Drain all the liquid and whole spices from the meat. Peel the garlic cloves, and, with the marinated meat, run through a meat grinder on a coarse setting. Mix the ground meat with the eggs, chopped truffles, pistachio nuts, duck glaze, truffle juice, salt and pepper to make a pâté.

Form pâté into twelve 2-inch balls. Top each with a small slice of foie gras and a thin slice of truffle. Cut the puff pastry into 4 pieces. Roll each piece into a strip, approximately 20-by-4-inches. Place 6 balls of pâté, spaced at 3-inch intervals, on two of the pastry strips. Brush egg wash on the pastry surrounding the pâté; cover with remaining sheets of pastry, pressing between the individual balls. Cut around each pâté with a large ring cookie cutter, pressing to seal the edges. Place the sealed pâtés on a buttered baking sheet. Decorate the tops with leftover puff pastry (using egg wash as "glue"); then brush with egg wash. Bake in a 425 degree oven for 10 to 15 minutes.

Place the pâtés on serving plates and ring with Sauce Perigueux (recipe follows).

SAUCE PERIGUEUX
1 onion, finely diced
1 carrot, finely diced
3 stalks celery, finely diced
¼ cup plus 1 tablespoon butter
1 quart Madeira
1 quart veal stock
1 ounce truffles, chopped
dash of cognac or Madeira
2 ounces foie gras, chopped
salt and pepper to taste

Sauté onion, carrot and celery in 1 tablespoon butter until lightly browned. Add Madeira and reduce to a glaze. Add the veal stock and reduce by one-half. Season to taste with salt and pepper. Strain through a fine mesh strainer or cheese cloth. Flame the truffle in the cognac. Add the truffle and foie gras to the sauce. Just before serving, add ¼ cup butter for extra flavor and shine.

SCALLOP MOUSSE

*½ pound fresh sea scallops (frozen
  will not work)*
1 ounce cognac
1 egg white
1½ cups heavy cream
salt and cayenne pepper to taste

Put scallops through a food grinder
twice. Transfer to a food processor
(see note below) and beat for 30 seconds with cognac, salt and cayenne
pepper; then add egg whites and
beat briefly. With machine running,
slowly add the heavy cream and process just until completely incorporated and mixture is smooth. (Do not
beat too long or mixture will separate.) Chill in the refrigerator for 2
hours.

   Note: If a food grinder is not available, purée scallops separately and
follow the remaining instructions.

HERB BUTTER SAUCE

1 quart white wine
8 ounces shallots, sliced
½ cup heavy cream
1 pound butter
juice of 1 lemon
1 large clove garlic
4 ounces fresh basil
2 ounces fresh chives
2 ounces watercress
4 ounces fresh parsley
4 ounces fresh tarragon
salt and cayenne pepper to taste

Reduce white wine with shallots to a
glaze. Add cream and reduce again
by one-half. Reduce heat to low and
add butter bit by bit, whisking constantly until completely incorporated.
Add lemon juice. Strain and adjust
seasoning with salt and cayenne pepper. Purée the garlic by hand; then
place it in a food processor and
purée with the fresh herbs. Add herb
purée one tablespoon at a time to the
butter sauce until the preferred color
and flavor is achieved. Reserve, keeping warm.

COURT BOUILLON

1½ quarts fish stock
1 shallot, sliced
½ quart white wine
2 bay leaves
6 black peppercorns
dash of salt

Combine the ingredients in a large
saucepan and bring to a boil. Reduce
heat to simmer and reserve.

ASSEMBLY

*8 Dover sole fillets, approximately 2
  ounces each*
1 lobster, about 1½ pounds, cooked
domestic sturgeon caviar
salmon caviar

Remove the shell of the boiled lobster
and slice the meat into medallions.
Reserve. Lay 2 Dover sole fillets side
by side (skinned-side up) on a buttered rectangle of aluminum foil.
Place the scallop mousse in a pastry
bag; then pipe mousse down the
seam of the fillets. Pipe a second
generous line of mousse on top of the
first. Fold fillets up and around the
mousse into the shape of a canoe.
Place medallions of lobster on top of
the mousse. Wrap the foil around the
fillets and seal securely. Place in the
court bouillon and simmer for 7 to 10
minutes. Remove from the foil and
serve immediately with herb butter
sauce. Garnish with both caviars.

Roast Breast of Pheasant Stuffed with Pheasant Mousse and Foie Gras

SERVINGS: 4
PREPARATION TIME: 1 HOUR (NOTE ELAPSED TIME)

PHEASANT MOUSSE
2 pheasants, 3 to 4 pounds each
1 ounce cognac
¾ cup heavy cream
½ ounce truffles, finely chopped
salt and white pepper to taste

Remove legs and breasts from pheasants. Bone and reserve breasts for assembly. Filet meat from thighs and legs. Put through a food grinder twice; then transfer to the work bowl of a food processor (see note below).

Process for 30 seconds with cognac and seasonings. With the machine running, slowly add the cream and process just until completely incorporated. When mixture is smooth, transfer to a smaller bowl and gently fold in truffles. Refrigerate for 2 hours.

Note: If a food grinder is not available, purée the leg meat separately in a food processor and continue with remaining instructions.

91

SHIITAKE MUSHROOM SAUCE

8 ounces shiitake mushrooms,
    stemmed and diced (other wild
    mushrooms may be substituted)
1 teaspoon butter
2 ounces cognac
1 pint heavy cream
3 tablespoons pheasant glaze (if
    unavailable, veal demi-glace will
    work: see page 99)
2 ounces butter (optional)
salt and pepper to taste

Briefly sauté the mushrooms in butter. Add cognac and flame. When
flame subsides, add cream to the
mushrooms and reduce briefly to
thicken. Add pheasant glaze. Taste
and adjust seasoning For extra shine
and flavor, add 2 ounces butter to the
sauce. Reserve, keeping warm.

ASSEMBLY

½ pound caul fat
4 ounces foie gras, cut into 4 baton-
    shaped strips
1 teaspoon butter
1 teaspoon oil
dash of cognac
½ cup white wine
salt and pepper

Soak caul fat in ice water for 1 hour.
Remove and pat dry. Cut into 4
6-inch squares. Make a slit lengthwise in each of the 4 reserved pheasant breasts, so that a pocket is
formed. Place each breast on a
square of caul fat. Fill each pocket
with about 2 tablespoons of pheasant mousse. Top the mousse with a
baton of foie gras. Close the breast
around the mousse and wrap each
breast with caul fat. Tie white string
around the breasts several times
lengthwise and widthwise. Season
both sides of the breasts with salt
and pepper. In an ovenproof sauté
pan, brown the breasts on both sides
in butter and oil. Transfer the pan to
a 400 degree oven and roast for 9 to
12 minutes. Remove the breasts from
the oven and let rest 3 to 4 minutes
before carving. Deglaze roasting pan
with cognac and wine and strain
juices into the mushroom sauce. Remove the strings and caul fat from
the breasts. Slice into medallions and
arrange on serving plates. Spoon
shiitake mushroom sauce around
the medallions and serve.

SERVINGS: 15-18
PREPARATION TIME: 1 HOUR (NOTE ELAPSED TIME)

1 quart milk
½ ounce powdered Japanese green tea
15 egg yolks
1 pound sugar
1 cup heavy cream
1 cup half and half

Bring milk to a boil. Remove from heat and add green tea. Mix well. In a separate bowl, beat egg yolks and sugar together until they form a ribbon. Combine egg mixture and milk, then strain into a saucepan. Cook over medium-high heat until just before the mixture reaches a boil. Remove from heat and cool completely over ice water. Beat heavy cream and half and half over ice water until frothy. Pour into egg mixture and mix well. Process in an ice cream maker according to manufacturer's instructions. Freeze for 2 to 3 hours before serving.

FRESH RASPBERRY SAUCE

1½ pints raspberries
1 cup sugar
1 cup water

Place all the ingredients in a saucepan. Bring to a boil and simmer for 15 minutes, stirring occasionally to break up raspberries. Purée in a food processor. Strain and cool in the refrigerator.

Serve spoonfuls of ice cream surrounded by raspberry sauce. Garnish plates with strawberries and slices of Japanese pears if desired.

JACKIE ETCHEBER
JACKIE'S

The green-and-white striped awning marking Jackie's is testimony to the validity of the American Dream: Jackie Etcheber arrived in the United States from her native Hong Kong thirteen years ago, at a mere 17, with just $1000 in her pocket. Twelve years later, she had acquired the skill and amassed the money to start her own restaurant, one that has received critical acclaim from the day it opened in September of 1982.

Jackie's original goal was not to be a chef, but to be a hotel manager back in Hong Kong. "My father thought I should be a secretary if I wanted to work, and then get married and have children. And my mother just thought I was crazy," she says. "So I asked my father for $1000, since I heard I could work as a waitress during the summer to support myself after the first year."

After a year at Ottumwa Heights College in Iowa, she transferred in 1973 to the hotel-management school at the University of Houston.

She moved to Chicago after graduation

in 1976, where she began as an assistant manager for a small restaurant in the Ritz-Carlton and met Pierre Etcheber, now her husband and the wine steward at Jean Banchet's famed Le Français. From the Ritz-Carlton she moved to the Park Hyatt, convincing them to allow her to switch from management to become steward of a kitchen.

The circuitous route to reaching her goal of owning a restaurant was taking the $4000 she saved and buying the lease for a seventeen-seat snack shop, dubbed Uncle Pete's. Jackie's break-even point was $60 a day, but she was soon doing five times that amount of business. And, she developed her hallmark of caring for customers individually, "I am very good with names and faces," she says, "People know if you're paying attention to them."

After eighteen months, she sold Uncle Pete's and, intent upon gaining the skills that would enable her to run a truly fine restaurant, went to work at La Mer, a seafood restaurant owned by Jean Banchet. Her next stop on the training circuit was Le Ciel Bleu. In the meantime, Pierre was investing her profits from the snack shop; by 1982 she had the money to buy Jackie's.

Diners are greeted by a panel of etched glass depicting lotus flowers and water lilies, echoed by a similar pattern above the bar. The walls are a pale gray; enlivening the mirrored wall at the far end of the sleek room is an arrangement of silk flowers.

Jackie talks rapidly as she works, and expects the staff to share both her drive and her hours. "I know I'm not the easiest person to work for, because I expect everyone to work as hard as I do." She arrives early each morning to supervise the kitchen cleaning and orders for the day, then cooks lunch and immediately begins dinner, finishing work around midnight.

The same personality that characterizes

Jackie's work carries over to the individual style of food that diners will find at her restaurant. Her predilection is toward seafood prepared with the light touch from her nouvelle French training, but many of the underlying flavors are drawn from her Chinese background.

"I love doing fish, and place most of my time on the nightly specials since I can get bored doing the same dishes too often," Jackie says. "I throw in Oriental ingredients and make discoveries in Chinese grocery stores. But I don't follow the methods of Chinese chefs. What I do is experiment and see what these ingredients can do to flavors when used in a Western-style restaurant."

"Creating them is like creating a painting," Jackie says. "I see colors as well as flavors, since the impressions of the dish begins when it arrives on the table, even before the first bite is eaten." ✗

JACKIE'S
CHICAGO

MENU

FILO NEST WITH EXOTIC MUSHROOMS
*Sautéed oyster mushrooms in a filo nest, garnished with snails, served with
tomato basil butter sauce*

HOT SEAFOOD SALAD
*Linguine, sautéed scallops and steamed mussels, garnished with goat's cheese and caviar,
served with mustard butter sauce*

STRIPED SEA BASS WITH SHRIMP, AVOCADO AND PEPPERS
Fillet of sea bass accompanied by shrimp and an array of colorful vegetables

QUAIL AND DUCK WITH RADICCHIO, MACHE AND GREEN PEPPERCORN SAUCE
*Roast quail on a lettuce bed, surrounded by sliced duck breast,
served with green peppercorn sauce*

CHOCOLATE BAG FILLED WITH WHITE CHOCOLATE MOUSSE
*A creamy white chocolate mousse and fresh strawberries in a delicate chocolate container, served
with raspberry sauce*

✗

SERVINGS: 4
PREPARATION TIME: 45 MINUTES

FILO NEST WITH EXOTIC MUSHROOMS

BEURRE BLANC SAUCE
  2 cups white wine
  10 large shallots, chopped
  2 tablespoons whipping cream
  2 pounds soft unsalted butter,
    quartered
  salt and pepper to taste

Combine wine and shallots in a
saucepan. Reduce to 1 tablespoon of
liquid. Add the cream and heat until
warm. Bit by bit, whisk in the butter.
Season with salt and pepper to taste.
Strain and reserve in a warm place
until use.

  Note: This recipe makes 4 to 5
cups and is the base for several
sauces that follow.

FILO NESTS
2 sheets of filo
salad oil
4 tablespoons bread crumbs

Cut each sheet in half. Fold each half sheet in half. Brush 4 soufflé molds, approximately 4 inches in diameter, with salad oil. Coat each mold with 1 tablespoon bread crumbs. Place one folded half sheet in each mold. Bake at 325 degrees for 10 minutes, checking frequently. Remove nests from molds and reserve.

MUSHROOMS AND SNAILS
2 tablespoons olive oil
½ pound oyster mushrooms, julienned
8 ounces bamboo shoots, chopped
½ finger ginger, julienned
2 scallions, chopped
1 clove garlic, minced
28 snails, shelled and rinsed
salt and pepper to taste

Heat 1 tablespoon of olive oil in a sauté pan. Add the mushrooms, bamboo shoots, ginger, scallions, ½ clove minced garlic and salt and pepper. Sauté until the mushrooms are tender. In another sauté pan, heat the remaining tablespoon of olive oil. Add the snails and ½ clove minced garlic. Season with salt and pepper and sauté just to warm. Reserve mushrooms and snails.

TOMATO BASIL BUTTER SAUCE
1-2 teaspoons tomato paste
3 leaves fresh basil, chopped
1 cup Beurre Blanc Sauce

Warm the tomato paste and basil in a saucepan. Whisk in the Beurre Blanc Sauce.

Place one filo nest on each serving plate. Fill the nests with the mushroom mixture. Garnish the plates with the sautéed snails. Spoon tomato basil butter sauce around the nests. If desired, place chopped tomato on top of the mushroom mixture.

SERVINGS: 4
PREPARATION TIME: 45 MINUTES

HOT SEAFOOD SALAD

MUSSELS
2 pounds extra large mussels
2 extra large shallots, chopped
1 cup white wine
1 tablespoon olive oil
salt and pepper to taste

Scrub the mussel shells. Rinse in cold water. Drain and combine mussels with the shallots and wine in a large saucepan. Cover and cook for about 5 minutes until the mussels open up and pull away from the shell. Remove mussels from shells. Debeard if necessary. Wash and reserve shells for garnish. Season and sauté the mussels in olive oil until lukewarm. Reserve, keeping warm.

SCALLOPS
1 tablespoon olive oil
1 pound sea scallops
1 tablespoon scallion, chopped
salt and pepper to taste

Heat olive oil in a sauté pan. Add the scallops, scallion, salt and pepper. Sauté scallops until warm and lightly browned. Reserve.

LINGUINE

1 pound linguine
1 tablespoon olive oil
salt and pepper to taste

Cook linguine in 3 to 4 quarts salted boiling water, al dente. Drain and sauté in olive oil. Season with salt and pepper. Reserve, keeping warm.

MUSTARD BUTTER SAUCE

1 teaspoon seed mustard
1 cup Beurre Blanc Sauce

Warm the mustard in a small saucepan. Whisk in the Beurre Blanc Sauce. Reserve, keeping warm.

ASSEMBLY

1 head radicchio, washed
¼ pound California goat cheese, cut in 4 pieces
4 teaspoons salmon caviar

In the center of each warm serving plate, place 1 leaf of radicchio. Place sautéed linguine on the leaf. Top with goat cheese and caviar. Arrange 4 mussel shells on each plate around the radicchio. Put 1 big mussel in each shell. Place scallops between the mussels. Garnish with any leftover mussels. To serve, spoon mustard butter sauce over the scallops and mussels and drizzle sauce over the linguine.

STRIPED SEA BASS WITH SHRIMP, AVOCADO AND PEPPERS

SERVINGS: 4
PREPARATION TIME: 30 MINUTES

---

4 striped sea bass fillets (with skin on for color), 8 ounces each
2 tablespoons olive oil
2 avocados, peeled, cored and sliced
juice of ½ lemon
12 shrimp (about 1 pound), peeled and deveined (or 2 pounds of whole shrimp)
1 green pepper, julienned
1 yellow pepper, julienned
1 red pepper, julienned
16 niçoise olives
12 miniature Italian yellow plum tomatoes
12 pattypan squash
salt and pepper to taste

Note: Halibut or red bass may be substituted for striped sea bass. Also, any colorful sautéed vegetables may substitute for the garnish suggested in this recipe.

Season the fillets with salt and pepper; sauté in 1 tablespoon olive oil, skin-side up, until flesh is no longer transparent. Place in a 400 to 450 degree oven for approximately 5 minutes. Peel, core and slice the avocados; then sprinkle with lemon juice. Sauté the remaining ingredients in 1 tablespoon olive oil just until shrimp are cooked. Place the sea bass fillets on serving plates. Top each with ½ of a sliced avocado. Surround the fillets with the sautéed shrimp and vegetables. Spoon lemon butter sauce (see recipe below) around the fillets and serve.

LEMON BUTTER SAUCE

1 teaspoon lemon juice
1 cup Beurre Blanc Sauce

In a small saucepan, warm the lemon juice. Whisk in the Beurre Blanc Sauce.

QUAIL AND DUCK WITH
RADICCHIO, MACHE
AND GREEN
PEPPERCORN SAUCE

VEAL DEMI-GLACE

20 pounds veal bones, browned
 3 medium onions, cubed or sliced
 2 medium carrots, sliced
 1 leek, diced
 3 stalks celery, cubed
 8 ounces tomato paste
 2 cups white wine

Place all of the ingredients in a 10-gallon stock pot. Fill pot with water and bring to a boil. Partially cover pot and simmer 18 hours, skimming constantly at the start and occasionally for the remaining cooking time. Strain and, only if necessary, reduce the stock until thick enough to coat a spoon. Makes approximately 8 cups. Demi-glace may be kept in the freezer indefinitely.

PEPPERCORN SAUCE

 3 tablespoons green peppercorns
 1 teaspoon shallot, diced
 1 tablespoon brandy
½ cup white wine
 4 cups veal demi-glace
 2 tablespoons soft butter (if desired)
salt and pepper to taste

Reduce green peppercorns, shallot, brandy and wine to 1 teaspoon of liquid. Add demi-glace and bring to a boil. Adjust seasoning. If desired, add butter just before serving to enrich the sauce. Reserve, keeping warm.

DUCK AND QUAIL

2 whole duck breasts, about ½ pound
 each
4 small quails, about 3 ounces each
1 tablespoon olive oil
1 head mache (lamb's lettuce)
1 head radicchio
salt and pepper to taste

Season the duck breasts on both sides with salt and pepper. Heat an ovenproof sauté pan to very hot. Place duck breasts in the pan, skin-side down, and briefly sauté. Place breasts in a 500 degree oven. After 1 minute, remove the pan and drain off fat. Return the pan to the oven for 2 to 3 minutes, until the skin is brown. Turn the breasts and cook a couple of minutes to medium rare, or preference. Remove breasts from oven and let rest 1 minute before slicing.

   In another ovenproof sauté pan, sauté the quail in olive oil until brown on both sides. Place in a 500 degree oven for approximately 4 minutes, turning once midway through cooking. On each serving plate, make a bed of mache and radicchio leaves. Place one quail on each lettuce bed. Slice the duck breasts with an electric knife. Arrange one-fourth of the duck, pinwheel fashion, on each serving plate. Spoon the green peppercorn sauce over the duck and serve.

Chocolate Bag Filled with White Chocolate Mousse

CHOCOLATE BAG WITH WHITE CHOCOLATE MOUSSE

SERVINGS: 12
PREPARATION TIME: 1 HOUR

MOUSSE

12 ounces white chocolate, chopped
1 cup milk
1 envelope (¼ ounce) unflavored gelatin
1 cup whipping cream
4 egg whites
squeeze of lemon juice

Melt the chocolate in the top of a double boiler over barely simmering water. In ¼ cup of milk, dissolve the gelatin.

Bring the remaining milk to a boil. In a bowl, gradually combine the melted chocolate and hot milk. Add the dissolved gelatin and stir until mixture is smooth and well-blended. Cool the mixture over a bowl of ice water, stirring occasionally until partially set.

Beat the whipping cream until stiff and refrigerate. Beat egg whites to soft peaks. Add the lemon juice; beat until stiff. Carefully fold together the whipped cream and egg whites. Gently add chocolate mixture. Refrigerate mousse overnight (or up to 3 days).

100

CHOCOLATE BAG

2½ pounds semi-sweet chocolate, melted

12 wax paper bages, approximately 3-inches wide and 8½ inches tall, with square bottoms (see note below)

Trim the top of the bag by half, to 4-inches tall. Open the bag, making sure that the bottom and sides are straight. Fold the top edge of the bag over so that the bag sits squarely. With a brush, "paint" the inside of the bag with melted chocolate. Repeat with all of the bags. Freeze overnight (bags will hold for 2 to 3 days in the freezer).

Note: 1 quart freezer bags can be adapted. Cut each bag to 5-inches tall and fold over top 2 inches. Open bag fully; tuck bottom corners under to form flat base. Secure with tape.

RASPBERRY SAUCE

16 ounces frozen raspberries

Grind raspberries in a food processor. Strain and refrigerate.

ASSEMBLY
fresh strawberries

Spoon chilled raspberry sauce onto serving plates. Just before serving, in a cool place, carefully peel the wax bag off the set chocolate. Spoon the white chocolate mousse into the chocolate bag and top with stemmed, halved strawberries. If desired, garnish with whipped cream, sliced kiwi and whole strawberries.

101

GREAT CHEFS OF CHICAGO WINE RECOMMENDATIONS

AMBRIA

CIGARETTES OF SMOKED SALMON WITH
BELUGA CAVIAR
Cremant des Moines Rosé Champagne (brut)

MOUSSE OF WILD MUSHROOMS WITH
LANGOUSTINES AND AMERICAN CAVIAR
Chateau Bouchaine Sauvignon Blanc

LOBSTER WITH THREE SALADS
Sonoma-Cutrer Chardonnay (Les Pierres Vineyards)

BREAST OF MALLARD ROTIS
Vega-Sicilia "Unico" Cabernet Sauvignon

POACHED PEAR STUFFED WITH ICE CREAM
*either Joseph Phelps late-harvest Johannisberg Riesling or
Taittinger Comtes de Champagne*

THE COTTAGE

SMOKED DUCK
Chalone Vineyard Pinot Noir

SEA SCALLOPS IN SPINACH LEAVES
Carmenet Sauvignon Blanc (Edna Valley)

"THE COTTAGE" SCHNITZEL
any nice Riesling Spatlese

"THE COTTAGE" RASPBERRY CAKE AND
CHOCOLATE RUM TERRINE
Mumm's non-vintage Cordon Rouge

PRINTER'S ROW

WILD MUSHROOMS FLAVORED WITH PINE
NEEDLES
Saki

NEW YORK DUCK LIVER TERRINE
Shramsberg or other domestic Champagne

FLUKE AND DAIKON
Sparkling water

VEAL DONE SIX WAYS
David Bruce or other California Pinot Noir

MACAROON MOCHA BUTTERCREAM CAKE
either late-harvest Riesling or botrytis-style Riesling

LE TITI DE PARIS

SAUSAGE OF SPINACH NOODLE
Muscadet (not older than six years)

SADDLE OF LAMB WITH FILET OF BEEF
Gigondas (six to 10 years old)

PROGRÈS WITH TWO CHOCOLATE MOUSSES
late-harvest Zinfandel

PEAR SOUFFLÉ
late-harvest Johannisberg Riesling

THE DINING ROOM

SALMON AND SEA BASS TERRINE
Beaujolais Blanc

QUAIL IN AN OMELET POUCH
Charmes Chambertin

TARTELETTE MIKADO
Chateau Mouton Rothschild

LAYERED LAMB CAKE
Chateau Haut Brion Blanc

WARM APPLE TART
Chateau Monbazillac

THE WINNETKA GRILL

GRILLED OYSTERS WITH SMOKED HAM AND
FRIED PARSLEY/BUTTERNUT SQUASH
RAVIOLI WITH ASIAGO CHEESE
*Iron Horse Brut Champagne, Kenwood Sauvignon Blanc
or a French white Graves*

MESQUITE ROAST LOIN OF PORK WITH APPLE
AND CORNBREAD STUFFING
*Iron Horse Pinot Noir, a young Gewurztraminer or a
light French Burgundy*

CHOCOLATE AND BOURBON PECAN CAKE
Essensia Orange Muscat (or similar Muscat)

LE VICHYSSOIS
SEAFOOD PÂTÉ IN BASIL SAUCE
Pouilly-Sur-Loire

SALMON BAKED IN PUFF PASTRY
Chablis Premier Cru

TARTE AU CHOCOLAT
Krug Brut Champagne

LE FRANÇAIS
SQUAB SALAD WITH WILD MUSHROOMS AND
QUAIL EGGS
Tavel Chateau de Manissy (or other Tavel Rosé)

LOBSTER WITH NOODLES, BASIL AND CAVIAR
Puligny Montrachet

ROAST SWEETBREADS WITH BELGIAN
ENDIVES AND TRUFFLES
*Batard-Montrachet or Pernard-Vergelesses Clos Berthet
Monopole*

NOISETTE OF VENISON WITH GRAND-VENEUR
SAUCE
Charmes-Chambertin

RASPBERRY FEUILLETE AND GRAND MARNIER
SOUFFLÉ
Taittinger Comtes de Champagne Rosé

CARLOS'
FLAN DE FOIE GRAS
Essensia Orange Muscat (or similar Muscat)

RAVIOLI OF LANGOUSTINE
Chassagne Montrachet

ASSIETTE OF SQUAB AND WILD MUSHROOMS
Chateau Lynch Bages

NIGHT AND DAY CAKE
Freemark Abbey Edelwein

FROGGY'S
SEAFOOD AND HERB SAUSAGE
Meursault

LOBSTER IN VANILLA SAUCE
Girard Chardonnay

BREAST OF DUCK WITH GREEN PEPPERCORN
SAUCE
Chateau Palmer

LEMON MOUSSE IN A PASTRY SHELL
Essensia Orange Muscat (or similar Muscat)

L'ESCARGOT
SNAIL TOURTE COUNTRY STYLE
Fetzer Fumé Blanc

MEDALLIONS OF VENISON WITH TRUFFLED
POTATOES
Clos-Vougeot

DESSERT IN ALL SIMPLICITY AND PEAR
CRÊPES
Taittinger Brut Champagne

YOSHI'S CAFÉ
HOT DUCK PÂTÉ
Jekel Johannisberg Riesling

DOVER SOLE WITH SCALLOP MOUSSE AND
MEDALLIONS OF LOBSTER
Chablis Grand Cru

ROAST BREAST OF PHEASANT STUFFED WITH
PHEASANT MOUSSE AND FOIE GRAS
Santenay

GREEN TEA ICE CREAM
Chateau Suduirat (Sauternes)

JACKIE'S
FILO NEST WITH EXOTIC MUSHROOMS
Sancerre

HOT SEAFOOD SALAD
Dopff and Irion Riesling (Alsace)

STRIPED SEA BASS WITH SHRIMP, AVOCADO
AND PEPPERS
Puligny-Montrachet

QUAIL AND DUCK WITH RADICCHIO, MACHE
AND GREEN PEPPERCORN SAUCE
Pommard

CHOCOLATE BAG FILLED WITH WHITE
CHOCOLATE MOUSSE
Chateau Suduirat (Sauternes)

The music for three of the Great Chefs series is performed by guitarist Charlie Byrd and his trio. Charlie has a distinguished career studded with many honors including an Emmy as a performer and music director for the Pageant of Performing Arts and numerous Down Beat magazine awards.

His latest album, "Brazilian Soul," has just been released on Concord Records. He also has a new mail order album out which is the instrumental soundtrack for THE GREAT CHEFS OF CHICAGO series entitled "Music To Dine By." Charlie continues to spend a portion of each year on the road, bring out new recordings, and write scores for films, television, modern dance and theatre.

Left to right, foreground: Frank Trapani, trumpet; Duke Barker, drums; Danny Rubio, tuba. Left to right, background: Frank Hooks, trombone; Phamous Lambert, piano; Mike Sizer, clarinet.

Food and music are synonymous with New Orleans, where the Great Chefs series originated, so naturally each of the Great Chefs shows opens and closes with the music of the world-famous Dukes of Dixieland.

The Dukes remain today one of the best proponents of New Orleans jazz. They perform nightly in their French Quarter nightclub, "Mahogany Hall." In the course of a year they present sixty concerts, appearing with major symphonies and festivals in the great concert halls of the world. They also record an album a year, their latest on Pro-Arte records entitled "Digital Dixieland." The Dukes are sponsored worldwide by Yamaha musical instruments and Paiste cymbals.

ACKNOWLEDGMENTS
✗

BOOK PRODUCTION
✗

TELEVISION PRODUCTION
✗

PUBLISHER	AVON BOOKS
PROPRIETORS	WYES-TV, NEW ORLEANS TELE-RECORD PRODUCTIONS LTD., NEW ORLEANS
EDITORIAL AND PRODUCTION SERVICES	JACK JENNINGS AND ANDREA CONNOLLY BMR, SAN FRANCISCO
WRITER	ELLEN BROWN Ms. Brown, author of *Cooking with the New American Chefs* (Harper & Row) is a freelance writer based in Washington, D.C. Formerly *food editor of USA Today,* Ms. Brown is now a food writer, restaurant critic and food industry consultant.
RECIPE EDITOR	TERRI HINRICHS
DESIGN	MICHAEL CRONAN DAVID CROSSMAN, BMR
CALLIGRAPHY	GEORGIA DEAVER
PHOTOGRAPHY	ERIC FUTRAN
PUBLIC RELATIONS	LINDA NIX, WYES-TV/NEW ORLEANS BILL MURRAY, WTTW-TV/CHICAGO BILL NATALE, WTTW-TV/CHICAGO CANDICE JACOBSON

WYES-TV/NEW ORLEANS

TELEVISION PRODUCER AND WRITER	JOHN BEYER
ASSOCIATE PRODUCER	TERRI HINRICHS
NARRATORS	MARY LOU CONROY ANDRES CALANDRIA
DIRECTOR	DAVE LANDRY
CAMERA	JIM LYNCH

WTTW-TV/CHICAGO

FIELD ENGINEER	ROY ALAN
FIELD AUDIO	ROBERT DOVE
KEY GRIP/GAFFER	REX VICTOR

TELE-RECORD PRODUCTIONS, LTD., NEW ORLEANS

MUSIC	CHARLIE BYRD TRIO THE DUKES OF DIXIELAND
TRANSPORTATION ENGINEER	ED NEER
EXECUTIVE PRODUCER	JOHN SHOUP
HEADQUARTER HOTEL FOR GREAT CHEFS PRODUCTION TEAM	THE RITZ-CARLTON

The best of
Chicago

à la Ritz!

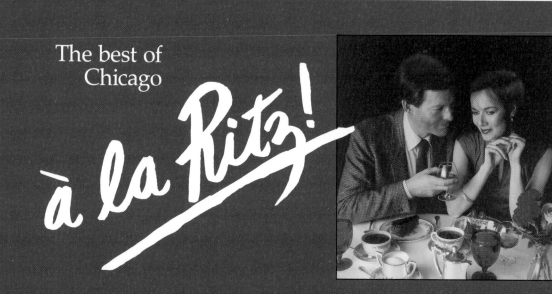

**The Ritz-Carlton Chicago
A Four Seasons Hotel
Proud Host and Official Hotel
for
"The Great Chefs of Chicago"
Salutes our Colleagues
for their Contributions to the
Culinary Arts**

THE RITZ-CARLTON
CHICAGO
at Water Tower Place
A Four Seasons Hotel

REORDER FORM
(please print)

☐ YES, I wish to order ____ additional copies of Chicago cookbooks at $9.95 each, plus $2.95 shipping and handling.

☐ YES, I wish to order ____ additional New Orleans II cookbooks at $9.95 each, plus $2.95 shipping and handling.

☐ YES, I wish to order ____ additional San Francisco cookbooks at $9.95 each, plus $2.95 shipping and handling.

☐ YES, I wish to order ____ additional New Orleans I cookbooks at $9.95 each, plus $2.95 shipping and handling.

TOTAL for my order is $_____

____ My check or money order is enclosed.

____ Charge my credit card.

     ____ Visa ____ Master Card

Account # _____ Expiration date _____

Signature _____

____ Please send further information.

____ Please send my gift order to the name and address I have provided.

Gift recipient: _____ _____

Address: _____

My name _____ Street _____

City _____ State _____ Zip code _____

PLEASE ALLOW FOUR WEEKS FOR DELIVERY

GREAT CHEFS, P.O. BOX 71112
NEW ORLEANS, LA 70172-9990
(504) 561-8323